Discovering
Tut-ankh-Amen's Tomb

SHIRLEY GLUBOK

Abridged and adapted from THE TOMB OF TUT-ANKH-AMEN
by HOWARD CARTER and A. C. Mace
Foreword by ERIC YOUNG, Associate Curator,
Department of Egyptian Art, The Metropolitan Museum of Art

Designed by Gerard Nook

MACMILLAN PUBLISHING CO., INC.
NEW YORK

The author gratefully acknowledges the cooperation and assistance of:

ALFRED H. TAMARIN

JOHN A. POPE, JR.

Other books by Shirley Glubok:

THE ART OF ANCIENT EGYPT

ART AND ARCHAEOLOGY

DIGGING IN ASSYRIA

DISCOVERING THE ROYAL TOMBS AT UR

THE ART OF CHINA

THE ART OF JAPAN

THE ART OF INDIA

THE ART OF THE SOUTHWEST INDIANS

THE ART OF THE PLAINS INDIANS

THE ART OF THE WOODLAND INDIANS

HOME AND CHILD LIFE IN COLONIAL DAYS

THE ART OF THE NEW AMERICAN NATION

THE ART OF THE OLD WEST

THE ART OF THE SPANISH IN THE UNITED STATES
AND PUERTO RICO

THE ART OF AMERICA SINCE WORLD WAR II

Macmillan Publishing Co., Inc.
866 Third Avenue, New York, N.Y. 10022
Collier Macmillan Canada, Ltd.
Library of Congress catalog card number: 68-12069
10 9 8 7 6
Printed in the United States of America

Discovering Tut-ankh-Amen's Tomb is abridged and adapted from *The Tomb of Tut-ankh-Amen*
by Howard Carter and A. C. Mace. Copyright © 1954 by Phyllis J. Walker. Used by permission
of Cooper Square Publishers, Inc., New York.

PICTURE CREDITS:
Ashmolean Museum (Harry Burton), 17, 20, 49, 61, 95;
Chicago Natural History Museum, 135 (right); *Illustrated London News*, 52;
F. L. Kenett, 6; Wide World Photos, 9, 29.
All other photographs by Harry Burton, courtesy of The Metropolitan Museum of Art.

Page 1 illustration: *Gold ceremonial stick showing
Tut-ankh-Amen at about twelve years of age*

Title page illustration: *Pectoral collar from the king's mummy*

Contents

Ba bird from the exterior trappings of the king's mummy

Gold statuette of Amenophis III

Foreword

"Above the Memnonium, in caves, are the tombs of the kings, which are rock-hewn, are about forty in number, are marvelously constructed, and are a spectacle worth seeing."

No modern tourist guide contains these words, but a book written about the time of Christ by the Greek geographer, Strabo. He is describing the Valley of the Kings on the west side of the Nile at Thebes, four hundred and fifty miles south of modern Cairo. Here, in rock-cut tombs, some hundreds of feet in length with fifteen or twenty chambers, were secretly buried most of the kings of Egypt of the Eighteenth, Nineteenth, and Twentieth dynasties. For four hundred years, from about 1500 to about 1100 B.C., funeral processions brought the fabulous wealth of royal treasuries to this remote valley to accompany the pharaohs in life after death.

Neither kings nor treasures were to remain undisturbed for long. Tomb robbing is one of the oldest professions in Egypt. From the time of Rameses IX (1142–1123 B.C.) we have the records of the trials of thieves who violated royal tombs, and the account of Strabo shows that by the first century B.C., and probably much earlier, most of the tombs were lying open, stripped of their furnishings, a source only of wonder for curious Greek tourists. The earliest modern traveler, Richard Pococke (1743), lists fourteen tombs. Many more were discovered in the nine-

teenth century, and the American explorer Theodore M. Davis discovered another fifteen between the years 1903 and 1909. With the last of these, the tomb of Hor-em-heb, it seemed that every king who should have been buried there was accounted for, and Davis sat back and said, "I fear that the Valley of the Tombs is now exhausted." Two Englishmen, Lord Carnarvon and Howard Carter, thought otherwise. The evidence for one particular tomb, that of Tut-ankh-Amen, was extremely flimsy.

Tut-ankh-Amen, reigning near the end of the Eighteenth Dynasty about 1350 B.C., was a shadowy figure about whom little was known. He was probably a son of Amen-hetep III and brother of Akh-en-Aten, born during a time of great political, religious, and social upheaval. His predecessor Akh-en-Aten is famous in history as the heretic pharaoh, promoter of the world's first attempt at monotheism—the worship of just one god. Egypt was a land with many gods, but at this time one particular god, Amen, reigned supreme. Amen was the local god of Thebes, and when Thebes came to prominence as the capital of Egypt, Amen was promoted to state god, king of all the gods. In the first half of the Eighteenth Dynasty Egyptian armies marched and fought to conquer an enormous empire. Spoils and tribute from conquered lands poured into Egypt and a large portion of this wealth was given by grateful kings to the god who made victory possible—Amen. The temples of Amen came to possess great wealth and the priests of Amen to wield great power, not only religious, but political, social, and economic.

To break this power Akh-en-Aten promoted the worship of the one god Aten, the disk of the sun. All other gods, and most particularly Amen, were proscribed, and the very name of Amen was wiped off the face of the land. The king's own name was changed from Amen-hetep to Akh-en-Aten in order to incorporate the name of the sun god. A new capital city, Akhetaten, was created at what is now called Amarna, some two hundred and fifty miles north of the Amen-dominated city of Thebes. Here the king, his family, and the favored ministers and officials of his court lived, worked, and were buried, or at least planned to be buried. And here, in one of the world's earliest examples of town planning, the young Tut-ankh-Amen, or Tut-ankh-Aten as he was then called, must have grown up.

When Akh-en-Aten died the great experiment died with him. Tut-ankh-Aten was a boy of about nine, completely under the control of the Amen priesthood and the powerful general Hor-em-heb. The young king was induced to change his name to Tut-ankh-Amen, to abandon the city of Akhetaten, and to return to Thebes. In his name the worship of Amen was completely reinstated, together with all the other gods. It was as if Akh-en-Aten had never existed.

Tut-ankh-Amen did not survive Akh-en-Aten for long. At the age of nineteen the last legitimate male heir of Amen-hetep III died, leaving a young widow, Ankh-es-en-Amen, an aging advisor, Ay, and the real power behind the throne, Hor-em-heb, to struggle for power. The insignificant king was buried in a small, hastily prepared tomb filled to overflowing with the furnishings of life and the equipment for death, all extremely modest when compared with what would have accompanied his illustrious predecessor, Thothmes III, or his own immediate fore-

bear, Amen-hetep III. This very insignificance, however, saved the tomb from serious violation while the furnishings of mightier pharaohs perished.

The finding and clearing of this tomb were described by Howard Carter in the three volumes of his book, *The Tomb of Tut-ankh-Amen*, and it is extracts from these volumes that are presented here. Many other books have been written about the tomb and its contents, but only the excavator himself, writing with the wonder of it fresh in his mind, can present the excitement, the tense expectation, the tedious labor, and the nerve-wracking responsibility of the work. Carter was to receive much assistance—more than thirty experts in various fields aided in preserving and studying the material, including no less than four members of the Metropolitan Museum of Art's own excavation staff in Egypt—but the final responsibility was his alone, while the entire world looked on. The world can consider itself lucky that these treasures were entrusted to a man who felt his responsibilities so keenly, and had the ability and character to carry the task to a successful completion. As Carter himself wrote, in a letter to Mrs. Robinson, wife of the one-time Director of the Metropolitan Museum of Art, "And I do not hesitate to tell you that when for the first time one enters a chamber such as this [the 'Treasury'], the sanctity of which has been inviolate for more than thirty centuries, an awe is felt, if not a fear, on the part of the intruder. It seemed almost desecrative to trouble that long peace and to break that eternal silence—a stillness intensified by the many inanimate things that filled it. Their very shadows seem to contain secrets of that tremendous past." If all excavators had felt this way, our knowledge of ancient Egypt would be many times greater than it is today.

ERIC YOUNG
*Associate Curator,
Department of Egyptian Art,
The Metropolitan Museum of Art*

*New York City
November, 1967*

Introduction

Howard Carter was born in England in 1873, the son of a painter who specialized in animal portraits. When he was seventeen young Carter was sent to Egypt with Professor Flinders Petrie's expedition, to make drawings of the excavations at Tell el-Amarna. There he first learned of the thrills and trials of excavating, and started his career as an archaeologist. As time went on he was appointed Chief Inspector of the Theban Necropolis and eventually met Lord Carnarvon, an art collector and amateur archaeologist who financed the Tut-ankh-Amen expedition.

Carter's three volumes, *The Tomb of Tut-ankh-Amen*, written shortly after the exploration of the tomb, give not only a firsthand account of the excavation, but also valuable information about how an archaeologist works. I have abridged the three volumes into a single book for young readers by cutting out some of the technical description and detail yet retaining the flavor and immediacy of Howard Carter's lively style. Since there is no consistency among Egyptian scholars in the spelling of proper names, these are being kept as Carter spelled them in his books. However, I have taken the liberty of changing verbs and common nouns from British to American usage.

It was most fortunate that the Egyptian Department of the Metropolitan Museum of Art sent Harry Burton, their expedition photographer, to Tut-ankh-Amen's tomb. Certainly some of his photographs are the best that have ever been taken of Egyptian excavations and artifacts. He took pictures during every step of the dig. Almost all of the photographs in this book were taken by him.

From the time that the tomb was discovered *Illustrated London News* featured the story. They were the first to show the individual objects as they were found, and theirs was the first real account of the excavation that came to the public.

There are many good books for further reading, but I would especially recommend Penelope Fox's *Tutankhamun's Treasure*, Christiane Desroches-Noblecourt's *Tutankhamen* for its beautiful pictures, and of course Carter's original three-volume work, *The Tomb of Tut-ankh-Amen*.

Shirley Glubok

New York City
November, 1967

Howard Carter

*Mirror case in the form
of the sign of life*

The Valley and the Tomb

The Valley of the Tombs of the Kings—the very name is full of romance, and of all Egypt's wonders there is none that makes a more instant appeal to the imagination. Here, in this lonely, valley head, remote from every sound of life, with the "Horn," the highest peak in the Theban hills, standing sentinel like a natural pyramid above them, thirty or more kings, among them the greatest Egypt ever knew, were buried.

Tucked away in a corner at the extreme end of the Valley, half concealed by a projecting basin of rock, lies the entrance to a very unostentatious tomb —that of Thothmes I. It has a special interest as the first ever constructed in the Valley. More than that: it is notable as an experiment in a new theory of tomb design.

To the Egyptian it was a matter of vital importance that his body should rest inviolate in the place constructed for it, and this the earlier kings thought to insure by erecting over the tomb a very mountain of stone.

It was also essential to a mummy's well-being that it should be fully equipped against every need, and, in the case of a luxurious and display-loving monarch, this would naturally involve a lavish use of gold and other treasure. The result was obvious. The very magnificence of the monument was its undoing. Within a few generations at most the mummy would be disturbed and the tomb's treasure stolen.

Various expedients were tried to protect the tomb: the entrance passage—naturally the weak spot—was plugged with granite monoliths weighing many tons; false passages were constructed; secret doors contrived; everything that ingenuity could suggest or wealth could purchase was employed. Vain labor, all of it, for by patience and perseverance the tomb robber in every case surmounted the difficulties set to baffle him. Moreover, success of these expedients, and therefore the safety of the tomb itself, was largely dependent on the good will of the mason who carried out the work, and the architect who designed it. Careless workmanship would leave a weakness in the best-planned defenses, and, in private tombs at any rate, an entrance for plunderers was sometimes contrived by the officials who planned the work.

At the beginning of the Eighteenth Dynasty (about 1600 years B.C.) there was hardly a king's tomb in the whole of Egypt that had not been rifled—a somewhat grisly thought to the monarch who was choosing the site for his own last resting place. Thothmes I evidently found it so, and devoted a good deal of thought to the problem. He decided on secrecy as the one chance of escaping the fate of his predecessors, and as a result built the lonely little tomb at the head of the Valley.

The early funerary monuments had always, in immediate proximity to the actual place of burial, a temple in which ceremonies were performed at various yearly festivals. Thothmes I decided there was to be no monument over the tomb itself, and the funerary temple in which the offerings were made was to be situated a mile or so away. It was certainly not a convenient arrangement, but it was necessary if the secrecy of the tomb was to be kept.

How long the secret of the tomb of Thothmes I held we do not know. Probably not long, for what secret was ever kept in Egypt? At the time of its discovery in 1899 little remained in it but the massive stone sarcophagus. The king himself had been moved, first of all to the tomb of his daughter Hat-shep-Sut, and subsequently with other royal mummies to Deir el-Bahari. In any case, whether the hiding of the tomb was temporarily successful or not, a new fashion had been set, and the remaining kings of the Eighteenth Dynasty, together with those of the Nineteenth and Twentieth, were all buried in the Valley.

For a few generations, under the powerful kings of the Eighteenth and Nine-

Approach to the Tombs of the Kings

teenth dynasties, the Valley tombs must have been reasonably secure. Plundering on a big scale would have been impossible without the connivance of the officials concerned. In the Twentieth Dynasty it was quite another story. There were weaklings on the throne, cemetery guardians became lax and venial, and a regular orgy of grave robbing seems to have set in.

Strange sights the Valley must have seen, and desperate the ventures that took place in it. One can imagine the plotting for days beforehand, the secret rendezvous on the cliff by night, the bribing or drugging of the cemetery guards, and then the desperate burrowing in the dark, the scramble through a small hole into the burial chamber, the hectic search by a glimmering light for treasure that was portable, and the return home at dawn laden with booty. We can imagine these things, and at the same time realize how inevitable it all was. By providing his mummy with the elaborate and costly outfit which he thought essential to his dignity, the king was himself compassing its destruction. The temptation was too great. Wealth beyond the dreams of avarice lay there at the disposal of whoever should find the means to reach it, and sooner or later the tomb robber was bound to win.

By the Twenty-first Dynasty, all attempts at guarding the tombs seem to have been abandoned, and the royal mummies were moved about from sepulcher to sepulcher in a desperate effort to preserve them. No fewer than thirteen of the royal mummies were moved at one time or another to the tomb of Amen-hetep II, and here they were allowed to remain. Other kings were eventually collected from their various hiding places, taken out of the Valley altogether, and placed in a well-hidden tomb cut in the Deir el-Bahari cliff. This was the final move, for by some accident the exact locality of the tomb was lost, and the mummies remained in peace for nearly three thousand years.

Throughout all these troubled times in the Twentieth and Twenty-first dynasties there is no mention of Tut-ankh-Amen and his tomb. He had not escaped altogether—his tomb having been entered within a very few years of his death—but he was lucky enough to escape the ruthless plundering of the later period. For some reason his tomb had been overlooked. It was situated in a very low-lying part of the Valley, and a heavy rainstorm might well have washed away all trace of its entrance. Or it may owe its safety to the fact that a number of huts, for use of workmen who were employed in excavating the tomb of a later king, were built immediately above it.

With the passing of the mummies the history of the Valley, as known to us from ancient Egyptian sources, comes to an end. Five hundred years had passed since Thothmes I constructed his modest little tomb there. From now on we are to imagine a deserted valley, spirit-haunted, doubtless, to the Egyptian, its cavernous galleries plundered and empty, the entrances of many of them open, to become the home of fox, desert owl, or colonies of bats.

In the early centuries of the Christian era, in the second to fourth centuries A.D., a colony of hermits was in full possession, used the open tombs as cells and transformed one into a church.

Magnificence and royal pride were replaced by humble poverty. The "precious habitation" of the king narrowed to a hermit's cell.

The Valley in Modern Times

For the first real description of the Valley in modern times we must turn to the pages of Richard Pococke, an English traveler who in 1743 published *A Description of the East*. Pococke gives an account of the tombs that were accessible at the time of his visit. He mentions fourteen in all, and gives the entire plan of five of the tombs. It is evident from Pococke's narrative that he was not able to devote as much time to his visit as he would have liked. The Valley was not a safe spot to linger in, for the pious hermit left in possession had given place to a horde of bandits who terrorized the whole countryside. These Theban bandits were notorious and we find frequent mention of them in the tales of eighteenth century travelers.

Let us now pass on to 1815. One of the most remarkable men in the whole history of Egyptology, a young Italian giant, Giovanni Battista Belzoni, spent five years in Egypt, excavating and collecting antiquities. He discovered and cleared a number of tombs in the Valley, including those of Ay, Mentu-her-khepesh-ef, Rameses I, and Seti I. This was the first occasion on which excavations on a large scale had ever been made in the Valley. Belzoni, like everyone else who has ever dug in the Valley, was of the opinion that he had absolutely exhausted its possibilities.

For twenty years after Belzoni's day, the Valley was well exploited. In 1844 the great German expedition under Karl Richard Lepsius made a complete survey of the Valley and cleared the tomb of Rameses II. Nothing more of any consequence was done in the Valley until the very end of the century.

In this period, however, just outside the Valley there occurred one of the most important events in the whole of its history. The various royal mummies had been collected from their hiding places and deposited all together in a rock cleft at Deir el-Bahari. There, for nearly three thousand years, they had rested, and there, in the summer of 1875, they were found by the members of a family in the village of Kurna, the Abd-el-Rasuls. It was in the thirteenth century B.C. that the inhabitants of this village first adopted the trade of tomb-robbing, and it is a trade that they have adhered to steadfastly ever since.

On this occasion the find was too big to handle. It was obviously impossible to clear the tomb of its contents, so the whole family was sworn to secrecy, and its heads determined to leave the find where it was, and to draw on it from time to time as they needed money. Incredible as it may seem the secret was kept for six years, and the family, with a banking account of forty or more dead pharaohs to draw upon, grew rich.

It soon became clear, from objects which came into the market, that there had been a rich find of royal material somewhere, but it was not until 1881 that it was possible to trace the sale of the objects to the Abd-el-Rasul family. One of its members made full confession. News was telegraphed at once to Cairo, Emile Brugsch Bey of the Cairo Museum was sent up to investigate and take charge, and on the fifth of July, 1881, the long-kept secret was revealed to him. It must have been an amazing experience. There, huddled together in a shallow, ill-cut grave, lay the most powerful monarchs of the ancient East, kings whose names were familiar to the whole world, whom no one in his wildest moments had ever dreamed of seeing. There they had remained, where the priests in secrecy had hurriedly brought them that dark night three thousand years ago; and on their coffins and mummies, neatly docketed, were the records of their journeyings from one hiding place to another. Some had been wrapped, and two or three in the course of their many wanderings had been moved to other coffins. In forty-eight hours—we don't do things quite so hastily nowadays—the tomb was cleared; the kings were embarked upon the museum barge; and within fifteen days of Brugsch

Bey's arrival at the Valley they were landed in Cairo and deposited in the museum.

As the barge made its way down the river the men of the neighboring villages fired guns as for a funeral, while the women followed along the bank, tearing their hair, and uttering that shrill quavering cry of mourning for the dead, a cry that has doubtless come down from the days of the pharaohs themselves.

To return to the Valley. In 1898, acting on information supplied by local officials, Victor Loret, then Director General of the Service of Antiquities, opened up several new royal tombs, including those of Thothmes I, Thothmes III, and Amen-hetep II. This last was a very important discovery. In the Twenty-first Dynasty thirteen royal mummies had found sanctuary in Amen-hetep's tomb and here, in 1898, the thirteen were found. It was but their mummies that remained. The wealth which they had lavished on their funerals had long since vanished.

The body of Amen-hetep still lay within its own sarcophagus, where it had rested for more than three thousand years. The Egyptian government decided against its removal. The tomb was barred and bolted, a guard was placed upon it, and there the king was left in peace.

In 1902 permission to dig in the Valley under supervision of the Egyptian government was granted to an American, Theodore Davis, and he subsequently excavated there for twelve consecutive seasons. His principal finds included the tombs of Thothmes IV, Hat-shep-sut, Si-Ptah, Yua and Thua (great-grandfather and grandmother of Tut-ankh-Amen's queen), Horem-heb, and a vault, not a real tomb, devised for the transfer of the burial of Akh-en-Aten from its original tomb at Tell el-Amarna. This cache included the mummy and coffin of Akh-en-Aten, a very small part of his funerary equipment, and portions of the sepulchral shrine of his mother, Tyi. In 1914 we acquired Mr. Davis's concession, and the story of the tomb of Tut-ankh-Amen really begins.

Valley of the Kings

17

Preliminary Work at Thebes

Theodore Davis had published the fact that he considered the Valley exhausted, and that there were no more tombs to be found, a statement corroborated by the fact that in his last two seasons he did very little work in the Valley proper, but spent most of his time excavating in the neighboring north valley. Nevertheless he was loath to give up the site, and it was not until June, 1914, that Lord Carnarvon and I actually received the long-coveted concession. Sir Gaston Maspero, Director of the Antiquities Department, who signed our concession, agreed with Mr. Davis that the site was exhausted.

We had made a thorough investigation of the site, and were quite sure that there were areas, covered by the dumps of previous excavators, which had never been properly examined. At the risk of being accused of hindsight, I will state that we had definite hopes of finding the tomb of one particular king, that of Tut-ankh-Amen.

This belief is explained by the published record of Mr. Davis's excavations. Toward the end of his work in the Valley he had found, hidden under a rock, a faience cup which bore the name of Tut-ankh-Amen. In the same region he came upon a small pit tomb, in which were fragments of gold foil, bearing the figures and names of Tut-ankh-Amen and his queen. On the basis of these fragments of gold he claimed that he had actually found the burial place of Tut-ankh-Amen. The theory was quite untenable, for the pit tomb in question was small and insignificant, ludicrously inadequate for a king's burial in the Eighteenth Dynasty. Some little distance eastward from this tomb, he had also found in one of his earlier years of work (1907–1908), buried in an irregular hole cut in the side of the rock, a cache of large pottery jars, with sealed mouths and hieratic inscriptions. A cursory examination was made of their contents, which seemed to consist merely of broken pottery, bundles of linen, and other oddments. Mr. Davis refused to be interested in them. The entire collection of jars was sent to the Metropolitan Museum of Art in New York. They proved extraordinarily interesting. There were clay seals, some bearing the name of Tut-ankh-Amen and others the impression of the Royal Necropolis Seal, fragments of magnificent painted pottery vases, linen head shawls—one inscribed with the latest known date of Tut-ankh-Amen's reign—floral collars of the kind represented as worn by mourners in burial scenes, and a mass of other miscellaneous objects; the whole apparently representing the material which had been used during the funeral ceremonies of Tut-ankh-Amen, afterward gathered together and stacked away within the jars.

We had thus three distinct pieces of evidence which seemed definitely to connect Tut-ankh-Amen with this particular part of the Valley. To these must be added a fourth. It was in the near vicinity of these other finds that Mr. Davis had discovered the famous Akh-en-Aten cache. This contained the funerary remains of heretic members of the royal family, brought hurriedly and hidden here for safety, and we can be reasonably sure that Tut-ankh-Amen was responsible for their removal and reburial because a number of his clay seals were found.

With all this evidence we were thoroughly convinced that the tomb of Tut-ankh-Amen was still to be found, and that it ought to be situated not far from the center of the Valley. We were in the act of completing our plans for an elaborate campaign in the seasons of 1914–1915 when war broke out, and for the time being all our plans had to be left in abeyance.

We resumed our work in this region in the season of 1919–1920. The idea was to clear the whole remaining part of the triangle of ground defined by the tombs of Rameses II, Mer-en-Ptah, and Rameses IV—the area in which we hoped the tomb of Tut-ankh-Amen might be situated—and we started in with

Lord Carnarvon

20

a fairly large gang of workmen. By the time Lord and Lady Carnarvon arrived in March the top debris had been removed, and we were ready to clear down into what we believed to be virgin ground below. We soon had proof that we were right, for we came upon a small cache containing thirteen alabaster jars, bearing the names of Rameses II and Mer-en-Ptah, probably from the tomb of the latter. As this was the nearest approach to a real find that we had yet made in the Valley, we were naturally excited, and Lady Carnarvon, I remember, insisted on digging out these jars—they were beautiful specimens —with her own hands.

With the exception of the ground covered by the workmen's huts, we had now exhausted the whole triangular area and had found no tomb. For our next attempt we selected the small valley in which the tomb of Thothmes III was situated. This occupied us throughout the whole of the two following seasons. Nothing intrinsically valuable was found.

We had now dug in the Valley for several seasons with extremely scanty results, and it became a much debated question whether we should continue the work or try for a more profitable site elsewhere. After these barren years were we justified in going on with it? My own feeling was that so long as a single area of untouched ground remained, the risk was worth taking. There was still the combination of flint boulders and workmen's huts at the foot of the tomb of Rameses VI to be investigated, and I had always had a kind of superstitious feeling that in that particular corner of the Valley one of the missing kings, possibly Tut-ankh-Amen, might be found. Certainly the stratification of the debris there indicated a tomb. Eventually we decided to devote a final season to the Valley, and, by making an early start, to cut off access to the tomb of Rameses VI, if that should prove necessary, at a time when it would least inconvenience visitors. That brings us to the present season.

Finding the Tomb

This was to be our final season in the Valley. Six full seasons we had excavated there, and season after season had drawn a blank; we had worked for months at a stretch and found nothing, and only an excavator knows how desperately depressing that can be. We had almost made up our minds that we were beaten, and were preparing to leave the Valley and try our luck elsewhere; and then hardly had we set hoe to ground in our last despairing effort than we made a discovery that far exceeded our wildest dreams. Surely, never before in the whole history of excavation has a full digging season been compressed within the space of five days.

Let me try and tell the story of it all. I arrived in Luxor on October 28 (1922) and by November 1st had enrolled my workmen and was ready to begin. Our former excavations had stopped short at the northeast corner of the tomb of Rameses VI, and from this point I started trenching southward. In this area there were a number of roughly constructed workmen's huts, used probably by the laborers in the tomb of Rameses. These huts, built about three feet above bedrock, covered the whole area in front of the Rameses side tomb and continued in a southerly direction to join up with a similar group of huts on the opposite side of the Valley. By the evening of November 3rd, we had laid bare a sufficient number of these huts for experimental purposes, so, after we had noted them, they were removed, and we were ready to clear away the three feet of soil that lay beneath them.

Hardly had I arrived next morning (November 4th) than the unusual silence, due to the stoppage of work, made me realize that something out of the ordinary had happened, and I was greeted by the announcement that a step cut in the rock had been discovered underneath the very first hut to be attacked. This seemed too good to be true, but a short amount of extra clearing revealed the fact that we were actually in the entrance of a steep cut in the rock, some thirteen feet below the entrance to the tomb of Rameses VI, and a similar depth from the present bed level of the Valley. The manner of cutting was that of the sunken stairway entrance so common in the Valley, and I almost dared to hope that we had found our tomb at last. Work continued feverishly throughout the whole of that day and the morning of the next, but it was not until the afternoon of November 5th that we succeeded in clearing away the masses of rubbish that overlay the cut, and were able to demarcate the upper edges of that stairway on all its four sides.

It was clear by now beyond any question that we actually had before us the entrance to a tomb, but there was always the horrible possibility that the tomb was an unfinished one, never completed and never used; if it had been finished there was the depressing possibility that it had been completely plundered in ancient times. On the other hand, there was just the chance of an untouched or only partially plundered tomb, and it was with ill-suppressed excitement that I watched the descending steps of the staircase as one by one they came to light. The cutting was excavated in the side of a small hillock, and, as the work progressed, its western edge receded under the slope of the rock until it was, first partially and then completely roofed in, and became a passage, ten feet high by six feet wide. Work progressed more rapidly now; step succeeded step, and at the level of the twelfth, toward sunset, there was disclosed the upper part of a doorway: blocked, plastered, and sealed.

A sealed doorway—it was actually true, then! Our years of patient labor were to be rewarded after all, and I think my first feeling was one of congratulation that my faith in the Valley had not been unjustified. With excitement growing to fever heat I searched the seal impressions on the door for evidence of the identity of the owner, but could find no name: the only decipherable ones were those of the Royal Necropolis Seal. Two facts were clear: first, the

employment of this royal seal was certain evidence that the tomb had been constructed for a person of very high standing; and second, that the sealed door was entirely screened from above by workmen's huts of the Twentieth Dynasty was sufficient proof that at least from that date it had never been entered.

While examining the seals I noted, at the top of the doorway where some of the plaster had fallen away, a heavy wooden lintel. Under this, to assure myself of the method by which the doorway had been blocked, I made a small peephole, just large enough to insert an electric torch, and discovered that the passage beyond the door was filled completely from floor to ceiling with stones and rubble—additional proof of the care with which the tomb had been protected.

It was a thrilling moment. I found myself, after years of comparatively unproductive labor, on the threshold of what might prove to be a magnificent discovery. Anything, literally anything, might lie beyond that passage, and I needed all my self-control to keep from breaking down the doorway and investigating then and there.

One thing puzzled me, and that was the smallness of the opening in comparison with the ordinary Valley tombs. The design was certainly of the Eighteenth Dynasty. Could it be the tomb of a noble buried here by royal consent or was it a royal cache, a hiding place to which a mummy and its equipment had been removed for safety? Or was it actually the tomb of the king for whom I had spent so many years in search?

Once more I examined the seal impressions for a clue, but only those of the Royal Necropolis Seal were clear enough to read. Had I known that a few inches lower there was a perfectly distinct impression of the seal of Tut-ankh-Amen, the kind I most desired to find, I would have cleared on, had a much better night's rest in consequence, and saved myself nearly three weeks of uncertainty. It was late, however, and darkness was already upon us. With some reluctance I reclosed the small hole that I had made, filled in our excavation for protection during the night, selected the most trustworthy of my workmen—themselves almost as excited as I was—to watch all night above the tomb, and so home to Luxor by moonlight, riding down the Valley.

Naturally my wish was to go straight ahead with our clearing, to find out the full extent of the discovery, but Lord Carnarvon was in England and in fairness to him I had to delay matters until he could come.

View of the royal cemetery (The entrance to the tomb of Tut-ankh-Amen is in the lower foreground, to the left of the boxes, behind the stone wall)

My next task was to secure the doorway against interference until such time as it could finally be reopened. This we did by filling our excavation up again to surface level, and rolling on top of it the large flint boulders of which the workmen's huts had been composed. By the evening, exactly forty-eight hours after we had discovered the first step of the staircase, this was accomplished. The tomb had vanished. So far as the appearance of the ground was concerned there had never been any tomb, and I found it hard at times to persuade myself that the whole episode had not been a dream.

I was soon to be reassured on this point. News travels fast in Egypt, and within two days of the discovery congratulations, inquiries, and offers of help descended upon me from all directions. It became clear that I was in for a job that could not be tackled singlehanded, so I wired to A. R. Callender, who had helped me on previous occasions, asking him, if possible, to join me without delay, and to my relief he arrived on the very next day.

On November 8th I had received a message from Lord Carnarvon, which read, "Propose arrive Alexandria twentieth."

We had nearly a fortnight, and we devoted it to making preparations. On the night of November 18th I went to Cairo, returning to Luxor on the 21st. On the 23rd, Lord Carnarvon arrived in Luxor with his daughter, Lady Evelyn Herbert, his devoted companion in all his Egyptian work, and everything was in hand for the beginning of the second chapter of the discovery of the tomb.

By the afternoon of the 24th the whole staircase was clear, sixteen steps in all, and we were able to make a proper examination of the sealed doorway. On the lower part the seal impressions were much clearer, and we were able without much difficulty to make out on several of them the name of Tut-ankh-Amen.

With heightened interest we renewed our investigation of the doorway. Here a disquieting element made its appearance. Now that the whole door was exposed to light it was possible to discern a fact that had hitherto escaped notice—there had been two successive openings and reclosings of a part of its surface. Furthermore the Royal Necropolis Seal originally discovered had been applied to the reclosed portions, whereas the sealings of Tut-ankh-Amen covered the untouched part of the doorway and were therefore those with which the tomb had been originally secured. The tomb then was not absolutely intact, as we had hoped. Plunderers had entered it, and entered it more than once—but that they had not rifled it completely was evident from that fact that it had been resealed.

Then came another puzzle. In the lower strata of rubbish that filled the staircase we found masses of broken potsherds and boxes bearing the names of Akh-en-Aten, Smenkh-ka-Re, and Tut-ankh-Amen, and, what was much more upsetting, a scarab of Thothmes III and a fragment with the name of Amen-hetep III. Why this mixture of names? The balance of evidence so far would seem to indicate a cache rather than a tomb, and at this stage we inclined more and more to the opinion that we were about to find a miscellaneous collection of objects of the Eighteenth Dynasty kings, brought from Tell el-Amarna by Tut-ankh-Amen, and deposited here for safety.

So matters stood on the evening of November 24th. On the following day the sealed doorway was to be removed so Callender set carpenters to work making a heavy wooden grille to be set up in its place. On the morning of the 25th the seal impressions on the doorways were carefully noted and photographed, and then we removed the actual blocking of the door, consisting of rough stones carefully built from floor to lintel and heavily plastered on their outer faces to take the seal impressions.

This disclosed the beginning of a descending passage (not a staircase), the same width as the entrance stairway, and nearly seven feet high. As I had already discovered from my hole in the doorway, it was filled completely with stone and rubble, probably the chip from its own excavation. This filling, like the doorway, showed distinct signs of more than one opening and reclosing of the tomb, the untouched part consisting of clean white chip, mingled with dust; whereas the disturbed part was composed mainly of dark flint. It was clear that an irregular tunnel had been cut through the original filling at the upper corner on the left side, a tunnel corresponding in position to the hole in the doorway.

The following day (November 26) was the day of days, the most wonderful that I have ever lived through, and certainly one whose like I could never hope to see again. Throughout the morning the work of clearing continued, slowly, on account of the delicate objects that were mixed with the filling. Then, in the middle of the afternoon, thirty feet down from the outer door, we came upon a second sealed doorway, almost an exact replica of the first. The seal impressions in this case were less distinct, but still recognizable as those of Tut-ankh-Amen and of the royal necropolis. Here again the signs of opening and reclosing were clearly marked upon the plaster. We were firmly convinced by this time that it was a cache that we were about to open, and not a tomb. We were soon to know. There lay the sealed doorway, and behind it was the answer to the question.

Slowly, desperately slowly it seemed to us as we watched, the debris that encumbered the lower part of the doorway was removed, until at last we had the whole door clear before us. The decisive moment had arrived. With trembling hands I made a tiny breach in the upper-left-hand corner. Darkness and blank space, as far as an iron testing rod could reach, showed that whatever lay beyond was empty. Candle tests were applied as a precaution against possible foul gases, and then, widening the hole a little, I inserted the candle and peered in, Lord Carnarvon, Lady Evelyn, and Callender standing anxiously beside me to hear the verdict. At first I could see nothing—the hot air escaping from the chamber caused the candle flame to flicker—but presently, as my eyes grew accustomed to the light, details of the room within emerged slowly from the mist: strange animals, statues, and gold—everywhere the glint of gold. For the moment—an eternity it must have seemed to the others —I was struck dumb with amazement, and when Lord Carnarvon, unable to stand the suspense any longer, inquired anxiously, "Can you see anything?" it was all I could do to get out the words, "Yes, wonderful things." Widening the hole a little farther so that we could both see, we inserted an electric torch.

Lady Evelyn, Lord Carnarvon, Howard Carter, and A. R. Callender

A Preliminary Investigation

Surely never before in the whole history of excavation had such an amazing sight been seen as the light of our torch revealed to us. Let the reader imagine how the objects in the tomb appeared to us as we looked down upon them from our spy hole in the blocked doorway, casting the beam of light from our torch—the first light that had pierced the darkness of the chamber for three thousand years—from one group of objects to another, in a vain attempt to interpret the treasure that lay before us. The effect was bewildering, overwhelming. I suppose we had never formulated exactly in our minds just what we had expected or hoped to see, but certainly we had never dreamed of anything like this, a roomful—a whole museumful it seemed—of objects, some familiar, but some the like of which we had never seen, piled one upon another in seemingly endless profusion.

Gradually the scene grew clearer, and we could pick out the individual objects. First, opposite to us—we had been conscious of them all the while, but refused to believe in them—were three great gilt couches, their sides carved in the form of monstrous animals, curiously attenuated in body, as they had to be to serve their purpose, but with heads of startling realism. Uncanny beasts to look upon; as we saw them, their brilliant gilded surfaces picked out of the darkness by our electric torch, as though by limelight, their heads throwing grotesque distorted shadows on the wall behind them, they were almost terrifying. Next, on the right, two statues held our attention: life-sized figures of kings facing each other like sentinels, black, gold-kilted, gold-sandaled, armed with mace and staff, the protective sacred cobras upon their foreheads.

These were the dominant objects. Between them, around them, piled on top of them, were countless others—exquisitely painted and inlaid caskets; alabaster vases, some beautifully carved in openwork designs; strange black shrines, a great gilt snake peeping out from the open door of one; bouquets of flowers or leaves; beds; beautifully carved chairs; a golden inlaid throne; a heap of curious white egg-shaped boxes; staffs of all shapes and designs; beneath our eyes, on the very threshold of the chamber, a beautiful lotus-shaped cup of translucent alabaster; on the left a confused pile of overturned chariots, glistening with gold and inlay; and peeping from behind them another portrait of a king.

Such were some of the objects that lay before us. Presently it dawned upon our bewildered brains that in all this medley of objects there was no coffin or trace of mummy, and the much-debated question of tomb or cache began to intrigue us afresh. We re-examined the scene before us and noticed for the first time that between the two black sentinel statues on the right there was another sealed doorway. The explanation gradually dawned upon us. We were but on the threshold of our discovery. What we saw was merely an antechamber. Behind the guarded door there were other chambers, possibly a succession of them, and in one of them, beyond any shadow of a doubt, in all his magnificent array of death, we should find the pharaoh lying.

We reclosed the hole, locked the wooden grille that had been placed upon the first doorway, left our guard, mounted our donkeys, and rode down the Valley, strangely silent and subdued.

We talked things over in the evening, to find that each of us had noticed something that the others had not, and it amazed us the next day to discover how many and how obvious were the things all of us had missed. Naturally, it was the sealed door between the statues that intrigued us most, and we debated far into the night the possibilities of what might lie behind it. A single chamber with the king's sarcophagus? That was the least we might expect. But why one chamber only? Why not a succession of passages and chambers,

Pages 32–33: *Interior of the Antechamber, southern end*

Pages 34–35: *Interior of the Antechamber, the Hathor couch*

Pages 36–37: *Interior of the Antechamber, northern end*

leading, in true Valley style, to an innermost shrine of all, the burial chamber? It might be so, and yet in plan the tomb was quite unlike the others. Visions of chamber after chamber, each crowded with objects like the one we had seen, passed through our minds. Then came the thought of the plunderers. Had they succeeded in penetrating this third doorway—seen from a distance it looked absolutely untouched—and, if so, what were our chances of finding the king's mummy intact? We slept but little that night.

Next morning there was much to be done. It was essential to have some more adequate means of illumination before proceeding. While this was in preparation we made careful notes of the seal impressions upon the inner doorways and then removed its entire blocking. By noon everything was ready and Lord Carnarvon, Lady Evelyn, Callender, and I entered the tomb and made a careful inspection of the first chamber, the Antechamber.

By the aid of our powerful electric lamps many things that had been obscure on the previous day became clear, and we were able to make a more accurate estimate of the extent of our discovery. Our first objective was naturally the sealed door between the statues, and here a disappointment awaited us. Seen from a distance it presented all the appearance of an absolutely intact blocking, but close examination revealed the fact that a small breach had been made near the bottom, just wide enough to admit a boy or a slightly built man, and that the hole had subsequently been filled up and resealed. We were not to be the first. Here, too, the thieves had forestalled us. It only remained to be seen how much damage they had had the opportunity to effect.

Our natural impulse was to break down the door, and get to the bottom of the matter at once, but to do so would have entailed serious risk of damage to many of the objects in the Antechamber, a risk which we were by no means prepared to face. Nor could we move the objects in question out of the way, for it was imperative that a plan and complete photographic record should be made before anything was touched, and this was a task involving a considerable amount of time, even if we had had sufficient equipment available—which we had not—to carry it through immediately. Reluctantly we decided to abandon the opening of this inner sealed door until we had cleared the Antechamber of all of its contents. By doing this we should not only insure the complete scientific record of the outer chamber which it was our duty to make, but we should have a clear field for the removal of the door-blocking, a ticklish operation at best.

Having satisfied to some extent our curiosity about the sealed doorway, we could now turn our attention to the rest of the chamber, and make a more detailed examination of the objects which it contained. It was certainly an astounding experience. Here, packed tightly together, were scores of objects, any one of which would have filled us with excitement under ordinary circumstances, and been considered ample repayment for a full season's work. Some were of types well enough known to us; others were new and strange, and in some cases these were complete and perfect examples of objects whose appearance we had heretofore but guessed at from the evidence of tiny broken fragments found in other royal tombs.

Nor was it merely in quantity that the find was so amazing. The period to which the tomb belongs is in many respects the most interesting in the whole history of Egyptian art, and we were prepared for beautiful things. What we were not prepared for was the astonishing vitality and animation which characterized certain of the objects. It was a revelation of unsuspected possibilities in Egyptian art, and we realized, even in this hasty preliminary survey, that a study of the material would involve a modification, if not a complete revolution, of all our old ideas.

One of the first things we noted in our survey was that all of the larger objects, and most of the smaller ones, were inscribed with the name of Tutankh-Amen. His, too, were the seals upon the innermost door, and therefore his, beyond any shadow of doubt, the mummy that ought to lie behind it. Next came a new discovery. Peering beneath the southernmost of the three great couches we noticed a small irregular hole in the wall. Here was yet another sealed doorway, and a plunderer's hole, which, unlike the others, had never been repaired. Cautiously we crept under the couch, inserted our portable light, and there before us lay another chamber, rather smaller than the first, but even more crowded.

The state of this inner room (afterward called the Annex) simply defied description. In the Antechamber there had been some sort of an attempt to tidy up after the plunderers' visit, but here everything was in confusion, just as they had left it. Nor did it take much imagination to picture them at their work. One—there would probably not have been room for more—had crept into the chamber, and had then hastily but systematically ransacked its entire contents, emptying boxes, throwing things aside, piling them one upon another, and occasionally passing objects through the hole to his companions for

Thoueris couch (Note plunderer's hole to the Annex)

clearer examination in the outer chamber. He had done his work just about as thoroughly as an earthquake. Not a single inch of floor space remained vacant. Beautiful things it contained, too, smaller than those in the Antechamber for the most part, but many of them of exquisite workmanship. Several things remain in my mind particularly—a painted box, apparently quite as lovely as the one in the Antechamber; a wonderful chair of ivory, gold, wood, and leatherwork; alabaster and faience vases of beautiful form; and a gaming board, in carved and colored ivory.

I think the discovery of this second chamber had a somewhat sobering effect upon us. For the first time we began to realize what a prodigious task we had in front of us, and what a responsibility it entailed. This was no ordinary find, to be disposed of in a normal season's work; nor was there any precedent to show us how to handle it. The thing was bewildering, and for the moment it seemed as though there were more to be done than any human could accomplish.

Moreover the extent of our discovery had taken us by surprise, and we were wholly unprepared to deal with the multitude of objects that lay before us, many in a perishable condition and needing careful preservative treatment before they could be touched. There were countless things to be done before we could even begin the work of clearing. Vast stores of preservatives and packing material had to be laid in; expert advice was needed as to the best method of dealing with certain objects; provision must be made for a laboratory—some safe and sheltered spot in which the objects could be treated, cataloged, and packed—a careful plan in scale had to be made and a complete photographic record taken while everything was still in position; a darkroom had to be contrived.

Clearly, the first thing to be done was to render the tomb safe against robbery; we could then work out our plans with easy minds. We had our wooden grille at the passage entrance, but that was not enough, and I measured the inner doorway for a gate of thick steel bars. Until we could get this made for us—for this and for other reasons it was imperative for me to visit Cairo—we must go to the labor of filling in the tomb once more.

On December 3rd, after closing up the entrance doorway with heavy timber, the tomb was filled to surface level. Lord Carnarvon and Lady Evelyn left on the 4th for England, to conclude various arrangements there, preparatory to returning later in the season; and on the 6th (leaving Callender to watch over the tomb), I went to Cairo to make my purchases. My first care was the steel gate, and I ordered it the morning I arrived, under promise that it should be delivered within six days. The other purchases I took more leisurely, photographic material, chemicals, a motor car, packing boxes of every kind, with thirty-two bales of calico, more than a mile of wadding, and as much again of surgical bandages.

While in Cairo I had time to take stock of the position, and it became more and more clear to me that assistance on a big scale was necessary if the work in the tomb was to be carried out in a satisfactory manner. The question was where to turn for this assistance. The first and pressing need was in photography, for nothing could be touched until a complete photographic record had been made, a task involving technical skills of the highest order. A day or two after I arrived in Cairo I received a cable of congratulations from Mr. Lythgoe, Curator of the Egyptian Department of the Metropolitan Museum of Art, New York, whose concession at Thebes was near ours, and in my reply I somewhat diffidently inquired whether it would be possible—for the immediate emergency, at any rate—to secure the assistance of Harry Burton, their photographic expert. He promptly cabled back, and his cable ought to go on record as an example of disinterested scientific cooperation: "Only too delighted to assist in any possible way. Please call on Burton and any other members of our staff."

This offer was subsequently most generously confirmed by the trustees and the director of the Metropolitan Museum, and on my return to Luxor I arranged with my friend Mr. Winlock, the director of the Metropolitan's excavations at Thebes, not only that Mr. Burton should be transferred, but that Mr. Hall and Mr. Hauser, draftsmen to the Metropolitan expedition, should devote such of their time as might be necessary to making a large-scale drawing of the Antechamber and its contents. Arthur C. Mace, director of the Metropolitan Museum's excavations on the pyramid field at Lisht, was also available. Thus no fewer than four members of the New York staff were associated in the work of the season. Without this generous help it would have been impossible to tackle the enormous amount of work in front of us.

Another piece of luck befell me in Cairo. A. Lucas, Director of the Chemical Department of the Egyptian Government, was taking three months' leave prior to retiring from the government, and he generously offered to place his chemical knowledge at our disposal for those three months, an offer I hastened to accept. That completed our regular working staff. In addition, Dr. Alan Gardiner kindly undertook to deal with any inscriptional material that might be found, and Professor James Henry Breasted gave us much assistance in the difficult task of deciphering the historical significance of the seal impressions from the doors.

I returned to Luxor and on December 16th we opened up the tomb once more. The next day the steel gate was set up in the door of the chamber and we were ready to begin work. On the 18th, work actually began, Burton making his first photographic experiments in the Antechamber, and Hall and Hauser starting on their plan. Two days later Lucas arrived, and at once began experimenting with preservatives for the various classes of objects.

On the 22nd, as the result of a good deal of clamor, permission was given to the press, both European and native, to see the tomb, and the opportunity was also afforded to a certain number of notables of Luxor, who had been disappointed at not receiving invitations to the official openings. On the 25th, Mace arrived, and two days later, photographs and plans being sufficiently advanced, the first object was removed from the tomb.

Visitors

Survey of the Antechamber

The Antechamber was a small room, some twenty-six by twelve feet, and we had to tread warily, for, though the officials had cleared a small alleyway in the center, a single false step or hasty movement would have inflicted irreparable damage on one of the delicate objects with which we were surrounded.

In front of us, in the doorway, lay the beautiful wishing cup. It was of pure semitranslucent alabaster, with lotus-flower handles on either side, supporting the kneeling figures which symbolize Eternity. Turning right as we entered, we noticed, first, a large cylindrical jar of alabaster; next, two funerary bouquets of leavens, one leaning against the wall, the other fallen; and in front of them, standing out in the chamber, a painted wooden casket. This last probably ranks as one of the greatest artistic treasures of the tomb. Its outer face was completely covered with gesso; upon this prepared surface there were a series of brilliantly colored and exquisitely painted designs—hunting scenes upon the curved panels of the lid, battle scenes upon the sides, and upon the ends representations of the king in lion form, trampling his enemies underfoot.

This was the first box we opened, and the ill-assorted nature of its contents

—to say nothing of the manner in which they were crushed and bundled together—was a puzzle. The reason for it became plain enough later.

Next, we came to the end (north) wall of the chamber. Here was the tantalizing sealed doorway, and on either side of it, mounting guard over the entrance, stood the life-size wooden statues of the king. They presented a painfully impressive appearance. Originally they were shrouded in linen shawls, and this must have added to the effect.

Turning now to the long (west) wall of the chamber, we found the whole of the wall space occupied by the three great animal-sided couches, curious pieces of furniture which we knew from illustrations in tomb paintings, but of which we had never seen actual examples. The first was lion-headed; the second cow-headed, and the third had the head of a composite animal, half hippopotamus and half crocodile. Each was made in four pieces for convenience in carrying, the actual bed frame fitting by means of hook and staple to the animals' sides, the animals' feet fitting into an open pedestal. As is usually the case in Egyptian beds, each had a foot panel but nothing at the head.

Beneath the lion-headed couch, resting on the floor, stood a large chest, made of a delightful combination of ebony, ivory, and redwood, which contained a number of small vases of alabaster and glass; two black wooden shrines, each containing a gilt figure of a snake, emblem and standard of the tenth province of Upper Egypt; a delightful little chair, too small for other than a child's use; two folding duckstools, inlaid with ivory; and an alabaster box, with incised ornamentation filled in with pigments.

The cow-headed couch was even more crowded. Standing on the floor in front of it were two wooden boxes. The larger box had interesting, varied contents. Thrown carelessly in were a number of faience cups, boomerangs mounted at either end with blue faience; a very elaborate tapestry-woven garment; and the greater part of a corselet. This last was composed of several thousand pieces of gold, glass, and faience.

The third couch was flanked by its pair of queer composite animals, with open mouths, and teeth and tongues of ivory. Below this couch stood another of the great artistic treasures of the tomb, a throne, overlaid with gold from top to bottom, and richly adorned with glass, faience, and stone inlay. Its legs, fashioned in feline form, were surmounted by lions' heads, fascinating in their strength and simplicity. Magnificent crowned and winged serpents formed the arms, and between the bars which supported the back were six protective cobras, carved in wood, gilded, and inlaid. It was the panel of the back, however, that was the chief glory of the throne, and I had no hesitation in claiming that it was the most beautiful thing that had yet been found in Egypt.

The scenes on the panel show one of the halls of the palace, a room decorated with flower-garlanded pillars, frieze of royal cobras, and dado of conventional "recessed" paneling. Through a hole in the roof of the palace the sun shoots down his life-giving protective rays. The king himself sits in an unconventional attitude upon a cushioned throne, his arm thrown carelessly

Painted casket in situ

Painted scene on the casket—
Tut-ankh-Amen hunting lions

46

across its back. Before him stands the girlish figure of the queen, apparently putting the last touches to his toilet: in one hand she holds a small jar of scent or ointment, and with the other she gently anoints his shoulder or adds a touch of perfume to his collar. A simple homely composition, but full of life and feeling and with such a sense of movement!

The coloring of the panel is extraordinarily vivid and effective. The face and other exposed portions of the bodies both of king and queen are of red glass, and the headdresses of brilliant turquoiselike faience. The robes are of silver, dulled by age to an exquisite bloom. The crowns, collars, scarves, and

other ornamental details of the panel are all inlaid with colored glass and faience, of carnelian, and of a composition hitherto unknown—translucent fibrous calcite, underlaid with colored paste. The background is the sheet gold with which the throne was covered. In its original state, with gold and silver fresh and new, the throne must have been an absolutely dazzling sight: now, toned down a little by the tarnishing of the alloy, it presents a color scheme still extraordinarily attractive and harmonious.

Apart from its artistic merit, the throne is an important historical document: the scenes upon it being actual illustrations of the politico-religious vacillations of the reign.

Before the couch were two stools, one of plain wood painted white, the other of ebony, ivory, and gold, its legs carved in the shape of ducks' heads, its top made in the semblance of leopard skin, with claws and spots of ivory— the finest example we know of its kind. Behind it, resting against the south wall of the chamber, there were a number of important objects. First came a shrine-shaped box with double doors, fastened by shooting bolts of ebony. This was entirely cased with thick sheet gold, and on the gold, in delicate low relief, there was a series of little panels depicting a number of episodes in the daily life of king and queen. Within the shrine there was a pedestal, showing that it had originally contained a statuette: it may well have been a gold one, an object, unfortunately, too conspicuous for the plunderers to overlook. It also contained considerable portions of the corselet already referred to.

A little farther along, peering out from behind the overturned body of a chariot was a statue of peculiar form, cut sharp off at waist and elbows. This was exactly life-size, and its body was painted white in evident imitation of a shirt; there can be very little doubt that it represents a mannequin to which the king's robes, and possibly his jeweled collars, could be fitted.

The rest of the south wall and the whole of the east, as far as the entrance doorway, were taken up by the parts of no fewer than four chariots. They were heaped together in terrible confusion, the plunderers having evidently turned them this way and that, in their endeavors to secure the more valuable portions of the gold decoration which covered them. Theirs was not the whole responsibility, however. The entrance passage was far too narrow to admit the complete chariots, so to enable them to get into the chamber the axles had been sawed in two, the wheels dismounted and piled together, and the dismembered bodies placed by themselves to facilitate their being carried in.

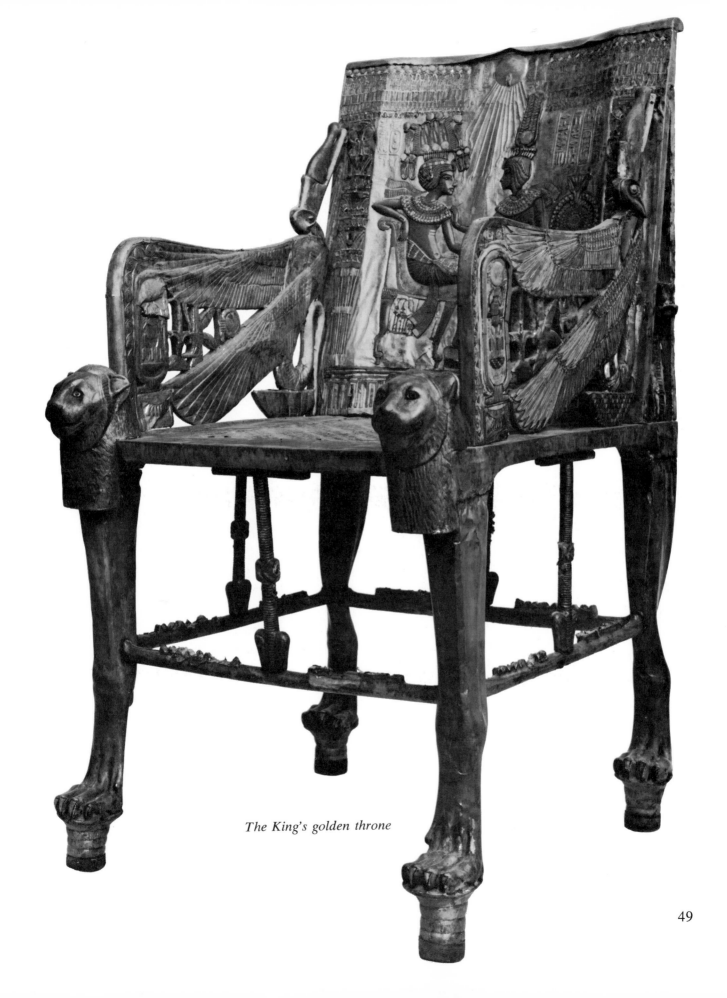

The King's golden throne

Clearing the Antechamber

Clearing the objects from the Antechamber was like playing a gigantic game of spillikens. So crowded were they that it was a matter of extreme difficulty to move one without running serious risk of damaging others. At such times life was a nightmare. We were afraid to move lest we should kick against a prop and bring the whole thing crashing down. Nor, in many cases, could we tell without experiment whether a particular object was strong enough to bear its own weight. Certain things were in beautiful condition, as strong as when they first were made, but others were in a most precarious state. The problem constantly arose whether it would be better to apply preservative treatment to an object *in situ*, or to wait until it could be dealt with in more convenient surroundings in the laboratory. The latter course was adopted whenever possible, but there were cases in which the removal of an object without treatment would have meant almost certain destruction.

It was slow work, painfully slow, and nerve-racking at that, for we felt a heavy weight of responsibility.

Granting that a heavy weight of responsibility must at all times rest upon the excavator, our own feelings will easily be realized. It had been our privilege to find the most important collection of Egyptian antiquities that had ever seen the light, and it was for us to show that we were worthy of the trust. So many things might go wrong: danger of theft, for instance. The whole countryside was agog with excitement about the tomb; all sorts of extravagant tales were current about the gold and jewels it contained; and it was only too possible that there might be a serious attempt to raid the tomb by night. This possibility of robbery on a large scale was negated, as far as possible, by a complicated guard system, there being present in the Valley, day and night, three independent groups of watchmen—the Government Antiquities Guards, a squad of soldiers supplied by the Mudir of Kena Province, and a selected group of the most trustworthy of our own staff—each answerable to a different authority. In addition, we had a heavy wooden grille at the entrance to the passage, and a massive steel gate at the inner doorway, each secured by four padlocked chains; and the keys were in the permanent charge of one particular member of the staff, who never parted with them for a moment, even to lend them to a colleague. Petty or casual theft we guarded against by doing all the handling of the objects ourselves.

Another cause of anxiety was the condition of many of the objects. With some of them their very existence depended on careful manipulation and correct preservative treatment.

There were other worries—visitors, for instance—and I fear that by the time the Antechamber was finished our nerves, to say nothing of our tempers, were in an extremely ragged state.

Obviously, our first and greatest need was photography. Before anything else was done, or anything moved, we had to have a series of preliminary views, taken in panorama, to show the general appearance of the chamber. For lighting we had available two movable electric standards, giving three thousand candlepower, and it was with these that all the photographic work in the tomb was done. Exposures were naturally rather slow, but the light was beautifully even, much more so than would have been afforded by flashlight— a dangerous process in such a crowded chamber—or reflected sunlight, the two possible alternatives. Fortunately, there was an uninscribed and empty tomb close by—the Davis cache tomb of Akh-en-Aten. We got permission from the government to use this as a darkroom, and there Burton established himself. It was not too convenient in some ways, but it was worthwhile to have a darkroom so close, for in the case of experimental exposures Burton could slip across and develop without moving his camera out of position.

Moreover, these periodic dashes of his from tomb to tomb must have been a godsend to the crowds of curious visitors who kept vigil above the tomb, for there were many days during the winter in which these were the only excitement they had.

Outside the tomb we had a difficult problem to solve, that of finding adequate working and storage space for the objects as they were removed. Three things were absolutely essential. First, we had to have plenty of room. Second, we had to have a thiefproof place, for as things were moved the laboratory would come to be almost as great a source of danger as the tomb itself. Last, we had to have seclusion. Eventually we solved the problem by getting permission from the government to take over the tomb of Seti II.

Thoueris couch being taken out of the tomb

One other point with regard to the laboratory work: we were five hundred miles from anywhere, and if we had run short of preservative materials there might have been considerable delay before we could secure a fresh supply. The Cairo shops furnished most of our needs, but there were certain chemicals of which we exhausted the entire Cairo stock before the winter was over. Constant care and forethought were necessary to prevent shortage and the consequent holding up of the work.

By December 27th all our preparations were made and we were ready to start on the actual removal of the objects. We worked on a regular system of division of labor. Burton came first with his photographs of the numbered groups of objects; Hall and Hauser followed with their scale plan of the chamber, every object drawn on the plan in projection; Callender and I did the preliminary noting and clearing and superintended moving the objects to the laboratory; and there Mace and Lucas received them, and were responsible for the detail noting, mending, and preservation.

The first object to be removed was the painted wooden casket. Then, working from north to south we gradually disencumbered the great animal couches of the objects which surrounded them. Each object was placed upon a padded wooden stretcher and securely fastened to it with bandages. From time to time, when a sufficient number of stretchers had been filled—once a day, on an average—a convoy was made up and dispatched under guard to the laboratory.

The removal and transport of the smaller objects was a comparatively simple matter, but it was quite otherwise when it came to the animal couches and the chariots. They were much too large to negotiate the narrow entrance passage, and must have been brought into the tomb in sections and assembled there. It was obvious that to get the couches out of the tomb we had to take them apart again; no easy matter, for after three thousand years the bronze hooks had naturally set tight in the staples and would not budge. We got them apart eventually, with scarcely any damage, but it took five of us to do it.

Most difficult of all to move were the chariots. Egyptian chariots are of very light construction, and the rough usage which they had undergone made these extremely difficult to handle.

It took us seven weeks in all to clear the Antechamber, and we were indeed thankful when it was finished without any kind of disaster befalling us. We had one scare. For two or three days the sky was very black, and it looked as though we were in for one of the heavy storms that occasionally visit Thebes. On such occasions rain comes down in torrents, and if the storm persists for any length of time the whole bed of the Valley becomes a raging flood. No power on earth could have kept our tomb from being flooded under these conditions, but, fortunately, though there must have been heavy rain somewhere in the district, we escaped with but a few drops.

In the course of our clearing we naturally accumulated a good deal of evidence with regard to the activities of the original tomb plunderers.

In the first place, we know from the sealings on the outer doorway that all the plundering was done within a very few years of the king's burial. We also know that the plunderer entered the tomb at least twice. It is just possible that the preliminary plundering was done immediately after the funeral ceremonies. Afterward, the passage was entirely filled with stones and rubbish, and it was through a tunnel excavated in the upper-left-hand corner of this filling that the subsequent attempt was made. At this final attempt the thieves had penetrated into all the chambers of the tomb, but their tunnel was only a narrow one, and clearly they could not have got away with any except the smaller objects.

There was a strange difference between the respective states in which the Antechamber and the Annex had been left. In the Annex, everything was in confusion, and there was not a vacant inch of floorspace. It was quite evident that the plunderers had turned everything topsy-turvy, and the present state of the chamber was precisely as they had left it. The Antechamber was quite different. There was a certain amount of confusion, but it was orderly confusion, and had it not been for the evidence of plundering afforded by the tunnel and the resealed doorways, one might have imagined at first view that there never had been any plundering, and that the confusion was due to carelessness at the time of the funeral.

However, when we commenced clearing it quickly became clear that this comparative orderliness was due to a process of hasty tidying-up, and that the plunderers had been just as busy in the Antechamber as they had in the Annex. Parts of the same object were found in different quarters of the chamber; objects that should have been in boxes were lying on the floor or upon the couches; there was a box lid behind the chariots, in an entirely inaccessible place, the box to which it belonged being far away, near the innermost door.

Later, when we came to unpacking the boxes we found still more circumstantial evidence. The long white box at the north end of the chamber was half full of sticks, bows, and arrows, and above, stuffed tightly in upon them, there was a mixed collection of the king's underlinen. In another box, jewelery and tiny statuettes had been packed on top of faience libation vases. Others, again, were half empty, or contained a mere jumble of odds and ends of cloth.

From the facts at our disposal, we could now reconstruct the whole sequence of events. A breach was first made in the upper-left-hand corner of the first sealed door, just large enough to admit a man, and then the tunneling began, the excavators working in a chain, passing the stones and baskets of

Convoy of antiquities to the laboratory

earth back from one to another. Seven or eight hours' work might suffice to bring them to the second sealed door; a hole in this, and they were through. Then in the semidarkness began a mad scramble for loot. Gold was their natural quarry, but it had to be in portable form, and it must have maddened them to see it glinting all around them on plated objects which they could not move, and had no time to strip. Nor, in the dim light, could they always distinguish between the real and the false, and many an object which they took for solid gold was found on closer examination to be but gilded wood, and was contemptuously thrown aside. The boxes were treated in very drastic fashion. They were all dragged into the center of the room and ransacked, their contents strewn all over the floor. What valuables the thieves found in them and made away with we may never know, but their search must have been hurried and superficial, for many objects of solid gold were overlooked. One very valuable thing they did secure. Within the small gold shrine there was a pedestal of gilded wood, made for a statuette, with the imprint of the statuette's feet still marked upon it. The statuette itself was gone and doubtless it had been a solid gold one.

The Antechamber having been thoroughly worked over, the thieves turned their attention to the Annex, knocking a hole in its doorway just big enough to let them through, and overturning and ransacking its contents quite as thoroughly as those of the Antechamber.

Then they directed themselves toward the burial chamber, and made a very small hole in the sealed doorway which screened it from the Antechamber. They may, indeed, have been disturbed at this particular stage in the proceedings. A very interesting little piece of evidence seems to bear this theory out. In the Antechamber one of the boxes contained a handful of solid gold rings tied up in a fold of cloth. They were just the thing to attract a thief, for their intrinsic value was considerable, and yet they could easily be hidden. Now, every visitor to Egypt knows that if you give money to a *fellah* [peasant] he would ordinarily proceed to undo a portion of his head shawl, put the coins in a fold of it, and finally secure it by looping the bag thus formed into a knot. This, unquestionably, was the work of one of the thieves. It was not his head shawl that he had used—the *fellah* of that period wore no such garment —but one of the king's scarves which he had picked up in the tomb, and he had fastened the coins thus for convenience in carrying. How, then, did it happen that the precious bundle of rings was left in the tomb and not carried off? It was the very last thing that a thief would be likely to forget, and, in the case of sudden alarm, it was not heavy enough to impede his flight, however hurried that might be. We are forced to conclude that the thieves probably were either trapped within the tomb, or overtaken in their flight—traced, in any case, with some of the plunder still upon them. This would explain the presence of certain other pieces of jewelery and goldwork too valuable to leave and too big to overlook.

In any case the fact that a robbery had been committed got to the ears of the officials, and they came to the tomb to investigate and make good the damage. For some reason they seem to have been in almost as great a hurry as the thieves, and their repairs were sadly inadequate. The Annex they left severely alone, not even taking the trouble to fill up the hole in the doorway. In the Antechamber the smaller objects with which the floor was covered were swept up, bundled together, and jammed back into the boxes, no attempt being made to sort the material, or to put the objects into the boxes for which they had been originally intended. Some of the boxes were packed tight, others were left almost empty. Nor was all the small material even gathered up. The larger objects were pushed carelessly back against the walls, or stacked one upon another. Certainly no respect was shown, either to the objects themselves or to the king whose property they were, and we wondered why, if they tidied up so badly, they took the trouble to tidy up at all. One thing we must credit them with: they did not do any pilfering as they might have done on their own account. We can be reasonably sure of that from the valuable objects, small and easily concealed, which they repacked into the boxes.

The Antechamber finished, the hole in the innermost doorway was refilled, plastered, and stamped with the Royal Necropolis Seal. Then, retracing their steps, the officials closed and sealed the Antechamber door, filled up the plunderers' tunnel through the passage blocking, and made good the outer doorway. What further steps they took to prevent repetition of the crime we do not know, but probably they buried the whole entrance to the tomb deep out of sight. In the long run nothing but ignorance of its whereabouts could have saved it from further attempts at plundering; and very certain it is that between the time of this reclosing and that of our discovery, no hand had touched the seals upon the door.

Duties of an Archaeologist

This chapter is dedicated to those—and they are many—who think that an excavator spends his time basking in the sun, pleasantly exhilarated by watching other people work for him, and otherwise relieved from boredom by having baskets full of beautiful antiquities brought up from the bowels of the earth from time to time for him to look at. His actual life is very different.

Every excavator must have a sense of responsibility. The things he finds are not his own property, to treat as he pleases, or neglect as he chooses. They are a direct legacy from the past to the present age, he is but the privileged intermediary through whose hands they come; and if, by carelessness, slackness, or ignorance, he lessens the sum of knowledge that might have been obtained from them, he knows himself to be guilty of an archaeological crime of the first magnitude. Destruction of evidence is so painfully easy, and yet so hopelessly irreparable. Tired, or pressed for time, he shirks a tedious piece of cleaning, or does it in a half-hearted, perfunctory sort of way, and he will perhaps have thrown away the one chance that will ever occur of gaining some important piece of knowledge.

Too many people—unfortunately there are so-called archaeologists among them—are apparently under the impression that the object bought from a dealer's shop is just as valuable as one which has been found in actual excavation, and that until the object in question has been cleaned, entered in the books, marked with an accession number, and placed in a tidy museum case, it is not at all a proper subject for study. There was never a greater mistake. Field work is all-important, and if every excavation were properly, systematically, and conscientiously carried out, our knowledge of Egyptian archaeology would be at least 50 per cent greater than it is. There are numberless derelict objects in the storerooms of our museums which would give us valuable information could they but tell us whence they came, box after box full of fragments, which could have been reconstructed if a few notes had been made when they were found. The first and most important rule in excavating is that the archaeologist must remove every antiquity from the ground with his own hands. So much depends upon it. Quite apart from the question of possible damage that might be caused by clumsy fingers, it is essential that he see the object *in situ*, to gain any evidence he can from the position in which it lies, and the relationship it bears to objects near it. For example, there may very likely be dating evidence. How many pieces there are in museums with vague "probably Middle Kingdom" kind of labels which, by reference to the objects with which they were found, might easily have been accurately assigned to the dynasty to which they belonged, or even to the reign of some particular king. There will also be evidence of arrangement, evidence that may show the use for which some particular object was made, or give the details for its ultimate reconstruction.

An excavator, then, must see every object in position, must make careful notes before it is moved, and, if necessary, must apply preservative treatment on the spot. Obviously, under these conditions it is all-important for him to keep in close touch with his excavations. Vacations and days off are out of the question. While the work is actually running he must be on the spot all day and available at all hours. His workmen must know where to find him at any given moment, and must have a perfectly clear understanding that the news of a discovery should be passed on to him without delay.

I suppose most excavators would confess to a feeling of awe—embarrassment almost—when they break into a chamber closed and sealed by pious hands so many centuries before. For the moment, time as a factor in human life has lost its meaning. Three thousand, four thousand years, maybe, have passed and gone since human feet trod the floor on which the archaeologist stands, and yet, as he notes the signs of recent life around him—the half-filled bowl of mortar for the door, the blackened lamp, the fingerprint upon the freshly painted surface—he feels it might have been but yesterday. The very air he breathes, unchanged throughout the centuries, he shares with those who laid the mummy to its rest. Time is annihilated by little intimate details such as these, and he is an intruder.

That is perhaps the first and dominant sensation, but others follow thick and fast—the exhilaration of discovery, the fever of suspense, the almost overmastering impulse, born of curiosity, to break down seals and lift the lids of boxes, the thought—pure joy to the investigator—that he is about to add a page to history, or solve some problem of research, the strained expectancy—why not confess it?—of the treasure seeker.

In the case of an important discovery the archaeologist will probably know something has happened before he actually gets the report, for—in Egypt, particularly—the news will have spread almost instantaneously, and have had a curious psychological effect upon the entire gang of workmen. They will be working differently, not necessarily harder, but differently, and much more silently. The ordinary work songs will have ceased. A smaller discovery can frequently be sensed in advance from the behavior of the man who brings the message. Nothing would induce him to come straight to the archaeologist and tell openly what he has found. At all costs he must make a mystery of it, so he hovers about in a thoroughly self-conscious manner, thereby advertising to the world at large exactly what has happened, and eventually makes himself still more conspicuous by beckoning the excavator aside and whispering his news. Even then it is difficult to get any but the vaguest reports out of him, and it will probably not be until the actual spot is reached that the archaeologist will find out exactly what has been found. This is due largely to an Egyptian's love of mystery for its own sake.

Most excavators work on what is known as the *baksheesh* [tipping] system: that is to say, they pay their workmen rewards, over and above their wages, for anything they find. It is not an ideal arrangement, but it has two advantages: it helps to insure the safety of the objects, particularly the small, easily concealed ones, which may be most valuable for dating purposes; and it makes the men keener about their work, and more careful about the manner in which they carry it out, the regard being more for the safe handling than for the value of the object.

Working on sentinal statue

For these and for many other reasons, it is all-important for the archaeologist to keep close to his work, and even if nothing is being found at the moment, he will not have much time to be idle. To begin with, every tomb, every building, every broken wall even, must be noted, and if he is dealing with pit tombs this may involve considerable gymnastic exercise. The pits may range anywhere from ten to a hundred and twenty feet in depth, and I calculated once that in the course of a single season I had climbed, hand over hand, up a half-mile of rope.

Then there is photography. Every object of archaeological value must be photographed before it is moved, and in many cases a series of exposures must be made to mark the various stages in the clearing. Many of these photographs will never be used, but the archaeologist can never tell when some question may arise, and a seemingly useless negative become a record of utmost value. Photography is absolutely essential, and it is perhaps the most exacting of all duties the excavator has to face. On a particular piece of work I have taken and developed as many as fifty negatives in a single day.

There are plenty of other jobs to be done, and the excavator's off hours and evenings will be very fully occupied if he is to keep up with his work. His notes, his running plans, and the registration of the objects must be kept thoroughly up to date. There are the photographs to be developed, prints to be made, and a register kept of negatives and prints. There will be broken objects to be mended, objects in delicate condition to be treated, restorations to be considered, and beadwork to be rethreaded. Then comes the indoor photography, for each individual object must be photographed to scale, and in some cases from several points of view. The list could be extended almost indefinitely, and would include a number of jobs that would seem to have but a remote connection with archaeology, such as account keeping, doctoring the men, and settling their disputes. The workmen naturally have one day a week off, and the excavator will very likely begin the season with the idea that he too will take a weekly vacation. He will usually be obliged to abandon the idea after the first week, for he will find in this day off too good an opportunity to waste of catching up with the hundred and one jobs that have got ahead of him.

Such is the life of the excavator. There are certain details of preservation work which we should like to dwell on at somewhat greater length.

Woodwork, for instance, is seldom in good condition and presents many problems. Damp and the white ant are its chief foes, and in unfavorable conditions nothing will be left of the wood but a heap of black dust or a shell which crumbles at the touch. In the one case, an entry in the notes to the effect that wood has been present is the most that can be done, but in the other there will generally be a certain amount of information to be gleaned. Measurements can certainly be secured; and the painted remains of an inscription, which may give the archaeologist the name of the owner of the object, and which a single breath of wind or touch of the surface would be sufficient to efface, can be copied, if taken in hand without delay. Again, there will be cases in which the wooden frame or core of an object was decayed, leaving scattered remains of the decoration—ivory, gold, faience, or what not— which originally covered its surface. By careful notes of the exact relative positions of this fallen decoration, supplemented by a subsequent fitting and piecing together, it will often be possible to work out the exact size and shape of the object. Then, by applying of the original decoration to a new wooden core, there results, instead of a miscellaneous collection of ivory, gold, and faience fragments, useless for any purpose, an object which for all practical purposes is as good as new. Preservation of wood, unless in the very last stage of decay, is always possible by application of melted paraffin wax; by this means an object which otherwise would have fallen to pieces can be rendered perfectly solid and fit to handle.

The condition of wood naturally varies according to the site, and, fortunately for us, Luxor was in this respect perhaps the most favorable site in all Egypt. We had trouble with the wood from Tut-ankh-Amen's tomb, but it arose, not from the condition in which we originally found it, but from subsequent shrinkage owing to change in atmosphere. This is not such a serious matter in an object of plain wood, but the Egyptians were extremely fond of applying a thin layer of gesso on which they painted scenes or made use of an overlay of gold foil. Naturally, as the wood shrank the gesso covering began to loosen and buckle, and there was considerable danger that large parts of the surface might be lost. The problem is a difficult one. It is a perfectly easy matter to fix paint or gold foil to the gesso, but ordinary preservatives will not fix gesso to wood. Here again, we had recourse eventually to paraffin wax.

The condition of textiles varies. Cloth in some cases is so strong that it might have come fresh from the loom, whereas in others it has been reduced by damp almost to the consistency of soot. In the present tomb the difficulty of

At work on the body of the chariot

64

handling it was considerably increased, both by the rough usage to which the garments had been subjected, and by the fact that so many of them were covered with a decoration of gold rosettes and beadwork.

Beadwork is in itself a complicated problem, and will perhaps tax an excavator's patience more than any other material with which he has to deal. The Eygptians were passionately fond of beads, and it is by no means exceptional to find upon a single mummy an equipment consisting of a number of necklaces, two or three collars, a girdle or two, and a full set of bracelets and anklets. In such a case many thousands of beads will have been employed.

In the recovery and restoration of this beadwork every single bead has to be handled at least twice. Very careful work is necessary to secure the original arrangement of beads. Restoration of missing or broken parts is sometimes necessary if a reconstruction is to be effected. Such restorations, based on actual evidence, are perfectly legitimate, and well worth the trouble.

For instance there were sandals of patterned beadwork of which the threading had entirely rotted away. As they lay on the floor of the chamber they looked in perfectly sound condition, but if we tried to pick one up it crumbled at the touch, and all we had for our pains was a handful of loose, meaningless beads. This was a clear case for treatment on the spot—a spirit stove, some paraffin wax, an hour or two to harden, and the sandal could be removed intact, and handled with the utmost freedom. Occasionally, particularly with the larger objects, it was found better to apply local treatment in the tomb just sufficient to ensure a safe removal to the laboratory, where more drastic measures were possible. Each object presented a separate problem, and there were cases in which only experiment could show what proper treatment was to be.

Papyrus is frequently difficult to handle. If it is in fairly sound condition it can be wrapped in a damp cloth for a few hours, and then it can easily be straightened out under glass. Rolls that are torn and brittle, sure to separate into a number of small pieces during the process of unwrapping, should never be tackled unless there is plenty of time and space available.

Stone, as a rule, presents few difficulties in the field. In the same way faience, pottery, and metal objects can usually be left for later treatment.

Detailed notes should be taken at every stage of this preliminary work.

Laboratory Work

Our laboratory was the tomb of Seti II that had been selected for us, and here we had established ourselves with our note cards and our preservatives. As the objects were brought in they were deposited, still in their stretchers, and covered up until they should be wanted. Each in turn was brought up to the working bay for examination. There, after the surface dust had been cleared off, measurements, complete archaeological notes, and copies of inscriptions were entered on file cards. The necessary mending and preservative treatment followed, after which the object was taken just outside the entrance for scale photographs. Finally the object was stored in the innermost recesses of the tomb to await the final packing.

Let us turn now to the individual treatment of a selected number of the antiquities. The first was the wonderful painted casket, and, if we had searched the whole tomb we should have been hard put to find a single object that presented a greater number of problems. Our first care was for the casket itself, which was coated with gesso and covered from top to bottom with brilliantly painted scenes. The surface dust was removed, the discoloration of the painted surfaces was reduced with benzine, and the whole exterior of the casket was sprayed to fix the gesso to the wood, particular attention being paid to tender places at the cracks. Three or four weeks later we noticed that the joint cracks were getting wider, and that the gesso in other places was showing a tendency to buckle. Owing to the change of temperature from the close, humid atmosphere of the tomb to the dry airiness of the laboratory, the wood had begun to shrink once more, and the gesso, not being able to follow it, was coming off from the wood altogether. Drastic measures were necessary, and we decided to use melted paraffin wax. We were thoroughly justified by the result, for the wax penetrated the materials and left everything firm, and, so far from the colors being affected, as we had feared, it seemed to make them more brilliant than before.

It will give some idea of the difficulty of handling this material if I explain that it took me three weeks of hard work to get to the bottom of the box. Immediately after the casket lid was removed and before anything had been touched, we noted that on the right there were a pair of rush and papyrus sandals in perfect condition; below them, just showing, a gilt head rest, and, lower again, a confused mass of cloth, leather, and gold. On the left, crumpled into a bundle, was a magnificent royal robe, and in the upper corner there were roughly shaped beads of dark resin. The robe presented us with our first problem, one that constantly recurred—how best to handle cloth that crumbled at the touch, and yet was covered with elaborate and heavy decorations.

This question of cloth and its treatment was enormously complicated by the rough usage to which it had been subjected. Had it been spread out flat or neatly folded, it would have been comparatively simple to deal with. We would, as a matter of fact, have had an easier task if it had been allowed to remain strewn about the floor of the chamber, as the plunderers had left it. Nothing could have been worse for our purposes than the treatment it had undergone in the tidying-up process, in which the various garments had been crushed, bundled, and interfolded, and packed tightly into boxes with a mixture of other and, in some cases, most incongruous objects.

In dealing with all these robes there were two alternatives before us. Something had to be sacrificed, and we had to make up our minds whether it should be the cloth or the decoration. It would be quite possible, by the use of preservatives, to secure large pieces of the cloth, but in the process we should inevitably have disarranged and damaged the bead ornamentation that lay below. On the other hand, by sacrificing the cloth, picking it carefully away piece by piece, we could recover, as a rule, the whole scheme of decoration. Later in the museum it would be possible to make a new garment of the exact size, to which the original ornamentation—beadwork, gold sequins, or whatever it may be—could be applied.

Returning to the casket—we began to explore its contents. With very few exceptions—the rush sandals are a case in point—the garments it contained were those of a child. Our first idea was that the king might have kept stored away the clothes he wore as a boy; but later, on one of the belts, and on the sequins of one of the robes, we found the royal cartouche. He must, then, have worn them after he became king, from which it would seem to follow that he was quite a young boy when he succeeded to the throne.

The most elaborate piece of reconstruction that we had to do was in connection with the corselet. This was very elaborate, consisting of four separate parts. Corselets of this type were evidently frequently worn, but we had never before been lucky enough to find a complete example. Unfortunately, the parts of it were sadly scattered, and there were points in its reconstruction of which we could not be absolutely certain.

Reconstruction of corselet

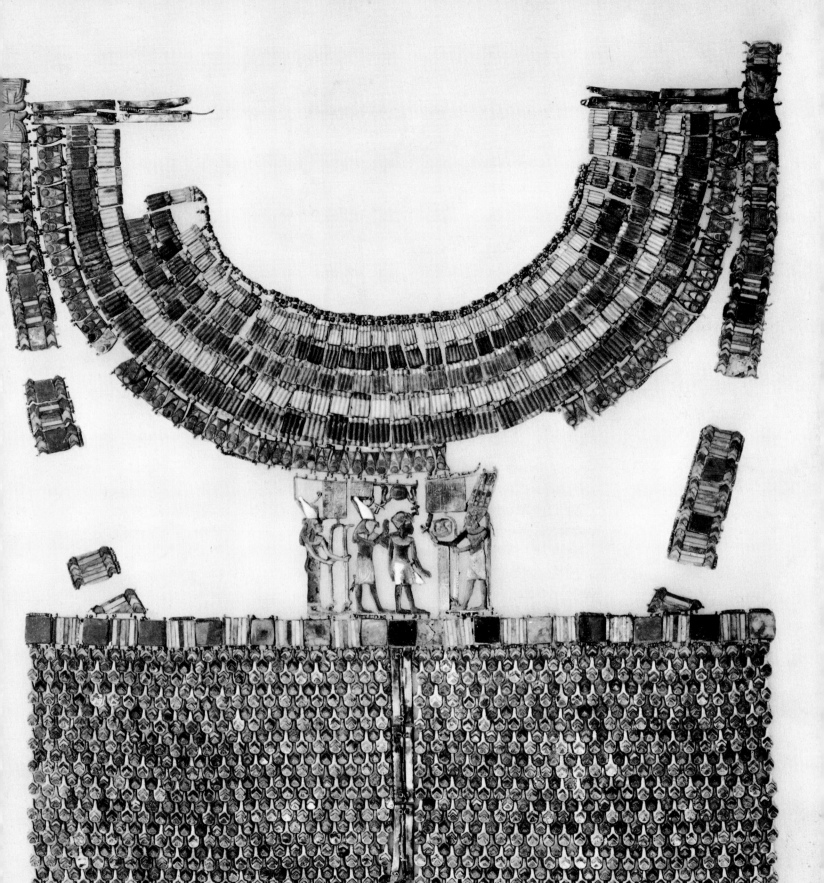

Opening the Sealed Door

By the middle of February, 1923, our work in the Antechamber was finished. With the exception of the two sentinel statues left for a special reason, all the contents had been moved to the laboratory, every inch of the floor had been swept and sifted for the last bead or fallen piece of inlay, and the room now stood bare and empty. We were ready at last to penetrate the mystery of the sealed door.

Friday, February 17th, was the day appointed, and at two o'clock those who were to be privileged to witness the ceremony met above the tomb. By a quarter past two the whole company had assembled and filed down the sloping passage into the tomb.

In the Antechamber everything was prepared and ready. We had screened the statues with boards to protect them from possible damage, and between them we had erected a small platform, just high enough to enable us to reach the upper part of the doorway, having determined it was safest to work from the top downward. A short distance back from the platform there was a barrier, and beyond, knowing that there might be hours of work ahead, we had provided chairs for the visitors. On either side of the doorway standards had been set up for our lamps, their light shining full upon the doorway.

There before us lay the sealed door, and with its opening we were to blot out the centuries and stand in the presence of a king who reigned three thousand years ago. My own feelings as I mounted the platform were a strange mixture, and it was with a trembling hand that I struck the first blow.

My first care was to locate the wooden lintel above the door: then I carefully chipped away the plaster and picked out the small stones which formed the uppermost layer of the filling. The temptation to stop and peer inside at every moment was irresistible. After about ten minutes' work, I had made a hole large enough to insert an electric torch. Its light revealed an astonishing sight, for there within a yard of the doorway, stretching as far as one could see and blocking the entrance to the chamber, stood what to all appearance was a solid wall of gold. For the moment there was no clue as to its meaning, so as quickly as I dared I set to work to widen the hole.

This had now become an operation of considerable difficulty, for the stones of the masonry were not accurately squared blocks built regularly upon one another, but rough slabs of varying size, some so heavy that it took all my strength to lift them. Many of them were left so precariously balanced that the least false movement would have sent them sliding inward to crash upon the contents of the chamber below. We were also endeavoring to preserve the seal impressions upon the thick mortar of the outer face, and this added considerably to the difficulty of handling the stones.

With the removal of a few stones the mystery of the golden wall was solved. We were at the entrance of the actual Burial Chamber of the king, and what barred our way was the side of an immense gilt shrine built to cover and protect the sarcophagus. It took us two hours of hard work to clear away the blocking, and at one point when near the bottom we had to stop for a while to collect the scattered beads from a necklace brought by the plunderers from within the chamber and dropped upon the threshold. This was a terrible trial to our patience, for it was a slow business, and we were all excited to see what might be within; but finally it was done, the last stones were removed, and the way to the innermost chamber lay open before us.

Fortunately, there were no smaller antiquities at this end of the chamber, so I lowered myself down, and then, taking one of the portable lights, I edged cautiously to the corner of the shrine and looked beyond it. At the corner two beautiful alabaster vases blocked the way, but I could see that if these were removed we should have a clear path to the other end of the chamber; so,

Pages 72–73: *Sentinel figures guarding shrine within the sepulcher*

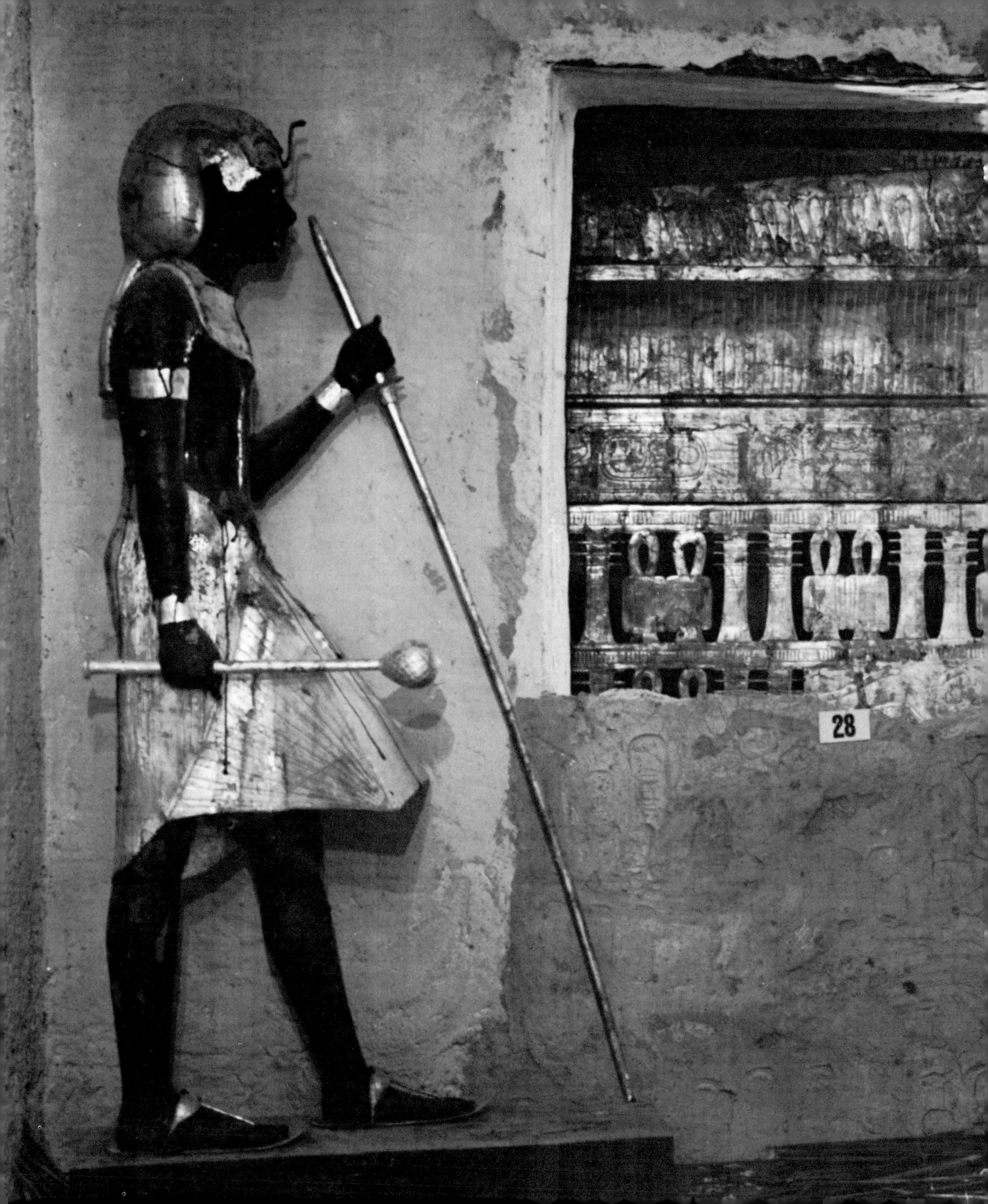
28

carefully marking the spot on which they stood, I picked them up and passed them back to the Antechamber. Lord Carnarvon now joined me, and, picking our way along the narrow passage between shrine and wall, paying out the wire of our light behind us, we investigated further. . . .

Towering above us was one of the great gilt shrines beneath which kings were laid. So enormous was this structure—seventeen by eleven feet, and nine feet high—that it almost filled the entire area of the chamber, a space of only two feet separating it from the four side walls, while its roof, with cornice top and torus molding, reached almost to the ceiling. From top to bottom it was overlaid with gold, and upon its sides there were inlaid panels of brilliant blue faience, in which were represented, repeated over and over, the magic symbols which would ensure its strength and safety. Around the shrine, on the ground, were a number of funerary emblems, and, at the north end, the seven magic oars the king would need to ferry himself across the waters of the underworld. The walls of the chamber, unlike those of the Antechamber, were decorated with brightly painted scenes and inscriptions, brilliant in their colors, but evidently somewhat hastily executed.

Our one thought was of the shrine and of its safety. Had the thieves penetrated within it and disturbed the royal burial? Here, on the eastern end, were the great folding doors, closed and bolted, but not sealed, that would answer the question for us. Eagerly we drew the bolts and swung back the doors, and there within was a second shrine with similar bolted doors, and upon the bolts, a seal intact. This seal we determined not to break, for our doubts were resolved, and we could not penetrate farther without risk of serious damage to the monument.

A feeling of intrusion had descended heavily upon us with the opening of the doors, probably heightened by the almost painful impressiveness of a linen pall, decorated with golden rosettes, which drooped above the inner shrine. We felt that we were in the presence of the dead king and must do him reverence, and in imagination we could see the doors of the successive shrines open one after another till the innermost disclosed the king himself. Carefully and as silently as possible we reclosed the great swinging doors, and passed on to the farther end of the chamber.

Here a surprise awaited us, for a low door, eastward from the Burial Chamber, gave entrance to yet another chamber, smaller than the outer ones and not so lofty. This doorway, unlike the others, had not been closed

The outermost (first) shrine

and sealed. We were able from where we stood to get a clear view of the contents, and a single glance sufficed to tell us that here within this little chamber lay the greatest treasures of the tomb. Facing the doorway, on the farther side, stood the most beautiful monument that I have ever seen—so lovely that it made me gasp with wonder and admiration. The central portion consisted of a large shrine-shaped chest, completely overlaid with gold and surmounted by a cornice of sacred cobras. Surrounding this, free standing, were statues of the four tutelary goddesses of the dead, gracious figures with outstretched protective arms, so natural and lifelike in their pose, the expression upon their faces so pitiful and compassionate that one felt it almost sacrilege to look at them. It was undoubtedly the Canopic chest and contained the jars which play such an important part in the ritual of mummification.

Immediately in front of the entrance to the small chamber lay the figure of the jackal god, Anubis, upon his shrine, swathed in linen cloth and resting upon a portable sled, and behind this, the head of a bull upon a stand—emblems of the underworld. On the south side of the chamber lay an endless number of black shrines and chests, all closed and sealed save one, whose open doors revealed statues of Tut-ankh-Amen standing upon black leopards. On the farther wall were more shrine-shaped boxes and miniature coffins of gilded wood. There were also a number of model boats with sails and rigging all complete, and, at the north side, yet another chariot.

We looked anxiously for evidence of plundering, but on the surface there was none. Unquestionably the thieves must have entered, but they cannot have done more than open two or three of the caskets. Most of the boxes had their seals still intact, and the whole contents of the chamber, in fortunate contrast to those of the Antechamber and the Annex, remained in position exactly as they had been placed at the time of burial.

How much time we spent in this first survey of the wonders of the tomb I cannot say, but it must have seemed endless to those waiting anxiously in the Antechamber. Not more than three at a time could be admitted with safety. It was curious, as we stood in the Antechamber, to watch their faces, as, one by one, they emerged. Each had a dazed, bewildered look in his eyes, and each in turn as he came out threw up his hands before him, an unconscious gesture of impotence to describe in words the wonders he had seen. It was an experience which none of us was ever likely to forget, for in imagination—and not wholly in imagination either—we had been present at the funeral ceremonies

Interior of the Innermost Treasury

Anubis guarding the entrance of the Innermost Treasury

The goddess Isis protecting the Canopic chest

79

of a king long dead and almost forgotten. At a quarter past two we had filed down into the tomb, and when, three hours later, hot, dusty, and disheveled, we came out once more into the light of day, the very Valley seemed to have changed for us and taken on a more personal aspect.

A week later, the tomb was closed and once again reburied. So ended our preliminary season's work on the tomb of Tut-ankh-Amen.

Packing, always an anxious business, was doubly so in this case owing to the enormous value of the material. Protection from dust as well as from actual damage was important, so every object was completely wrapped in cottonwool or cloth, or both, before it was placed in its box. Delicate surfaces, such as the parts of the throne, the legs of the chairs and beds, or the bows and staffs, were swathed in narrow bandages, in case anything should work loose in transit. Very fragile objects, like the funerary bouquets and the sandals, which would not bear ordinary packing, were laid in bran husks. Eighty-nine boxes in all were packed, but to lessen the danger in transit these were enclosed within thirty-four heavy packing cases.

Then came the question of transport. At the riverbank a steam barge was waiting, but between the laboratory and the river stretched a distance of five and one-half miles of rough road, with awkward curves and dangerous slopes. Three possibilities of transport were open to us—camels, hand portage, and the railway—and we decided on the third as least likely to jar the cases. They were loaded on a number of flat cars, and by the evening of May 13th they were ready to begin their journey down the Valley, the road by which they had passed, under such different circumstances, three thousand years before.

In the coming winter our first task, a difficult and anxious one, would be the dismantling of the shrines in the sepulchral chamber. How long this work would take we could not tell, but it had to be finished before we tackled the innermost chamber of all, and we could count ourselves lucky if we could accomplish the clearing of both in a single season. A further season would surely be required to clear the Annex, with its confused jumble of contents.

One shadow rested upon the work, one regret, which all the world must share—the fact that Lord Carnarvon died in April, 1923, and never saw the fruition of his work. In completion of that work we who carried it out dedicated to his memory the best that lay in us.

Howard Carter preparing a statue of the king for transport to the laboratory

The Tomb and Burial Chamber

Instead of the orthodox Theban plan—an elaborate series of corridors, sunken staircases, protective well and vestibule, farther descending passages, antechamber, sepulchral hall, crypt, and series of four storerooms—Tut-ankh-Amen's tomb merely comprises a sunken entrance staircase, a descending passage, an antechamber with annex, a burial chamber and one storeroom, all small and of the simplest kind. In fact, it only conforms with the Theban pattern of the New Empire royal tomb in orientation, by having its burial chamber alone painted gold and by having in its walls niches for the magical figures of the four cardinal points.

In orientation the Burial Chamber, as well as its nest of four shrines, sarcophagus, coffins, and mummy, runs east-west, accurate to within four degrees of magnetic north. The doors of the shrines, in accordance with the guide marks on them, were intended to face west, but for reasons not altogether clear they were actually erected facing east: had the shrines been placed in their correct and intended orientation, access to their folding doors might have been most difficult, and their purpose constricted in that very small chamber, as it would have been well nigh impossible to have introduced objects such as were found between the outermost and second shrines.

In shape, the Burial Chamber is rectangular, having its long axis at right angles to that of the Antechamber. The walls of the Burial Chamber were coated with a gypsum plaster, and were painted yellow. The rock ceiling was left plain, in its rough and unfinished state. It is interesting that traces of smoke, from an oil lamp or torch, are visible upon the ceiling in the northeast corner.

The construction of the partition wall dividing the Antechamber from the Burial Chamber and the plastering and decoration of the chamber itself must have taken place after the burial of the king, the closing of the sarcophagus, and the erection of the four shrines. The plastering and painting that covered the inner face of the partition wall was uniform with the rest of the decoration, so the plastering and painting of the entire chamber must necessarily have been done after the erection of the shrines, under exceptionally difficult conditions and in a very confined space, which may account for the crudeness of the workmanship.

The subjects treated in the painting upon the walls are of funerary and religious import. One scene is unprecedented: the figure of the reigning king, Ay, presiding over the obsequies (burial rites) of his dead predecessor.

Depicted on the east wall is a scene of the funeral procession: the deceased Tut-ankh-Amen, upon a sledge, is being drawn by courtiers to the tomb. The mummy is shown supported upon a lion-shaped bier, within a shrine, on a boat which rests upon the sledge. The bier painted here resembles that actually found in the sarcophagus under the coffins, while the shrine is of similar design to that which encloses the Canopic chest and jars in the storeroom of the tomb. Over the dead king are festoons of garlands; on the boat in front of the shrine is a sphinx rampant; before and behind the shrine are the mourning goddesses Nephthys and Isis; and attached to the prow and stern of the boat, as well as on both sides of the shrine, are red and white pennants. The courtiers and high officials forming the cortege are divided up in the following order: a group of five nobles, two groups of two nobles each, two officials wearing garments such as distinguish the viziers, and, lastly, a courtier. Each wears upon his wig or bare-shaven head, as the case may be, a white linen fillet such as is usually found in funeral processions illustrated in private tomb chapels, and like those still used by the modern Egyptian on such occasions to distinguish relatives and retainers of the deceased's household.

On the north wall, east corner, is a scene of historical importance showing

Ay as King, with royal insignia, clad in a leopard's skin of the *Sem* priest. Here King Ay officiates at the funeral ceremony of "The Opening of the Mouth" of the dead Tut-ankh-Amen represented as Osiris. Between the living and the dead monarchs are the objects connected with the ceremonial laid out upon a table: the adze, a human finger, the hind limb of an ox, the fan of a single ostrich feather, and a double plumelike object. These are surmounted by a row of five gold and silver cups containing what may be balls of incense such as found in the Antechamber.

In the center of the north wall Tut-ankh-Amen, wearing a wig, fillet, and white kilt, stands before the goddess Nût. The third scene, at the west end of the wall, refers to the king's spiritual rather than his bodily form: it shows Tut-ankh-Amen followed by his *Ka* [spirit] embracing Osiris.

When we entered the Burial Chamber we found, lying beside a small hole made by the robbers through the masonry of the door which had been subsequently reclosed by the ancient Egyptian officials, portions of two necklaces

Burial Chamber—north wall decoration

dropped by a thief. Standing in the southeast corner was a lamp resting upon a trellis-work pedestal, carved out of pure translucent calcite. Its chalicelike cup, which held the oil and a floating wick, was not decorated either on its exterior nor interior surface, yet when the lamp was lit the king and queen were seen in brilliant colors within the thickness of its translucent stone. At first we were puzzled as to how this ingenius effect was accomplished. Perhaps the explanation is that there were two cups turned and fitted, one within the other. A picture had been painted in semitransparent colors, on the inner cup, and was visible only through the translucent outer cup when the lamp was lit.

Beneath this unique lamp, wrapped in reeds, was a silver trumpet, which, though tarnished with age, would still fill the Valley with a resounding blast. Standing along the east wall was Amen's sacred goose of wood, varnished black, and swathed in linen; beside it were two rushwork baskets collapsed with age, and a wine jar bearing the legend: "Year 5, wine of the house of (?)

Tut-ankh-Amen, from the Western river Chief of the Vintners, Kha."

Resting upon the ground, between the shrine and the north wall of the Burial Chamber, were magic oars to ferry the king's barque across the waters of the netherworld, and with them, one at each end, curious devices in varnished black wood. At the western end of the chamber, in the northern and southern corners, were golden emblems of Anubis hung on lotus-shaped poles, standing erect, in alabaster pots placed upon reed mats. They may belong to the dark world under the earth, where the sun sinks, and where, also, the dead sleep: perhaps, emblems to guide the dead through this domain, for was not Anubis—the jackal—a prowler of the dusk, and did not Re send him forth to bury Osiris?

When we drew back the ebony bolts of the great shrine, the doors swung open as if closed only yesterday, and revealed yet another shrine, like the first save for a blue inlay. It had similar bolted doors, but upon them was a seal intact bearing the name of Tut-ankh-Amen and a recumbent jackal over Egypt's nine foes. Above the shrine drooped a linen pall. This bespangled pall, brown with age, still hanging on its curious wooden supports, was rent by the weight of the gilt bronze daisies sewn to its fabric. The shrine, dazzling from the brilliance of its gold, was decorated in beautiful incised relief with scenes from the book "of that which is in the Underworld"—that guide to the Hereafter, which points out to the deceased the road he should take, and explains to him the various evil powers he must meet during his subterranean journey. According to this book two routes, one by water, the other by land, led the deceased to the land of the blessed.

The pall made us realize that we were in the presence of a dead king of past ages. The unbroken seal upon the closed doors of the second shrine gave us the data we were seeking. The shrine was intact, indicating that the robbers had not reached him. Henceforth, we knew that, within the shrine, we should be treading where no one had entered, and we should be dealing with material untouched and unharmed since the boy king was laid to rest nearly 3,300 years ago. We had at last found what we never dreamed of attaining—an absolute insight into the funerary customs in the burial of an ancient pharaoh.

In front of the second shrine's doors stood the king and queen's perfume vase, carved of pure semitranslucent alabaster, a rare masterpiece of intricate stone carving embellished with gold and ivory. In front of this beautiful object, partially covered by fallen portions of the pall, stood another powerful

Howard Carter at the door of the second shrine

piece of conventional art. This was a cosmetic jar, of various kinds of carved calcite, which still contained its cosmetic.

On either side, between the two shrines, stacked in the right and left corners, were numerous ceremonial maces, sticks, staffs, and bows, some carefully wrapped in linen. Perhaps the choicest of them all were the gold and silver sticks, made of two thin tubular shafts supporting tiny statuettes of the king, cast and chased in their respective metals. Save for their metals, they are exactly alike and are clearly the products of a master hand.

A series of curved batons were most elaborately decorated. Among other sticks was a plain reed mounted with broad gold and electrum rings and plaited gold wire. We wondered why such an ordinary, plain reed should have been so richly mounted, but the legend written upon it gave the touching solution: "A reed which His Majesty cut with his own hand."

Such were the appointments in the Burial Chamber, all of them expressing a fine art in the service of superstition. The whole chamber and its appointments beautifully represented the mentality of those ancients. Mingled with a fear of the very gods and demons of their own creation one is conscious of sincere feeling and affection for the dead. Its appointments, like those of the Antechamber, may almost be divided into two categories: the personal and the religious—the personal objects reflecting the tastes of the young king, the religious objects reflecting the superstitions of the past.

But the problems here suggested are difficult. The meaning of some of the emblems placed in the tomb may have been almost as obscure to the ancient Thebans as to ourselves. The true significance of the symbols might well have been lost years before the age of Tut-ankh-Amen and tradition may have held them to be necessary for the welfare of the dead long after the reason for their use had been forgotten.

Besides the traditional paraphernalia necessary to meet and vanquish the dark powers of the netherworld, there were magical figures placed in small recesses in the walls, facing north, south, east, and west, covered with plaster, conforming with the ritual laid down in the Book of the Dead for the defense of the tomb and its owner. Magic, for once, seems to have prevailed. For of twenty-seven monarchs of the imperial age of Egypt buried in this valley, who have suffered every kind of depredation, Tut-ankh-Amen alone, throughout those thirty-three centuries, had lain unscathed.

258

Magical figure of Anubis

Clearing the Burial Chamber and Opening the Sarcophagus

The second season's work actually began in the laboratory, under Mr. Mace, who dealt with the magnificent chariots and the ceremonial couches that were left over from the first season. While he was carrying out this work of preservation and packing, with the aid of Mr. Callender, I began by removing the two guardian statues that stood before the doorway of the Burial Chamber, and then, as it was necessary, demolished the partition wall dividing it from the Antechamber.

The demolition of the partition wall gave a clear view of the great outermost shrine, and we were able to realize its grandeur, especially its admirable goldwork and blue faience inlay, overlaid with gilt protective emblems—*Ded,* the amulet of Osiris, and *Thet,* the knot of Isis—alternately.

Beyond the very limited space and high temperature which prevailed, our difficulties were further increased by the great weight of the various sections and panels of which those complex shrines were constructed. These were made of two-and-a-quarter-inch oak planking, overlaid with superbly delicate goldwork upon gesso. The wood planking, though perfectly sound, had shrunk in the course of 3,300 years in that very dry atmosphere, the goldwork upon the gesso had slightly expanded; the result was a space between the basic wood and the ornamented gold surface which, when touched, tended to crush and fall away. We had to deal in that very limited space with those sections of the shrines, weighing from a quarter to three-quarters of a ton, without causing them undue damage.

The outermost shrine, occupying nearly the whole Burial Chamber, measured some seventeen feet in length, eleven feet in width, and over nine feet in height. The four shrines comprised in all some eighty sections, each section or part having to be dealt with differently, and every section first needing to be temporarily treated to allow it to be handled without the least risk of damage.

The next procedure was to remove and transport to the laboratory all the portable funerary equipment that had been placed around the chamber between the walls and the sides of the outermost shrine, and then introduce the necessary scaffolding and hoisting tackle preparatory to dismantling the outermost shrine. Our gear, necessarily primitive, being placed in position, we began by first unhanging the very heavy folding doors of this shrine. This was a very tedious and hazardous task. Then the panels of the shrine had to be removed.

The next and very delicate problem was the linen pall that completely covered the second shrine. Its tissue was much decayed and in very fragile state; its drooping edges were badly torn from the weight of its own material, and by the metal daisies that were sewn to it. Happily, duroprene proved most effective in reinforcing the deteriorated fabric. It strengthened the tissues sufficiently to enable us to roll the fabric onto a wooden roller, expressly made for the purpose, and transport it to the laboratory where eventually it would be treated and relined.

The linen pall disposed of, we were able to study the second shrine—a beautiful gilt construction almost exactly similar to the first, save for the absence of the blue faience inlay. The doors of this second shrine were bolted top and bottom, carefully fastened with cord tied to metal staples, and sealed. The clay seal upon this cord was intact. It bore impressions of two distinct seals, one bearing Tut-ankh-Amen's personal name, surmounting a jackal over nine foes, the second bore the Royal Necropolis Seal. Behind those two seals we would be dealing with material unharmed since the burial of the king. It was with great care that the cords were severed, those folding doors opened to reveal yet a third shrine, also sealed and intact—the seal impressions upon this third shrine being identical to those on the second shrine.

I carefully cut the cord, removed that precious seal, drew back the bolts, and opened the door. A fourth shrine was revealed, similar in design and even more brilliant in workmanship than the last. The decisive moment was at hand! An indescribable moment for an archaeologist! What was beneath and what did that fourth shrine contain? With intense excitement I drew back the bolts of the last and unsealed doors; they slowly swung open and there, filling the entire area within, stood an immense yellow quartzite sarcophagus intact, with the lid still firmly fixed in its place, just as the pious hands had left it. It was certainly a thrilling moment as we gazed upon the spectacle enhanced by the striking contrast—the glitter of metal—of the golden shrines shielding it. Especially striking were the outstretched hand and wing of a goddess sculptured on the end of the sarcophagus, as if to ward off an intruder. It symbolized an idea beautiful in conception, and, indeed, seemed an eloquent illus-

Below: *Second shrine, fastened and sealed*
Right: *The innermost (fourth) shrine*

tration of the perfect faith and tender solicitude for the well-being of their loved ones that animated the people who dwelt in that land over thirty centuries ago.

The three remaining shrines had to be taken to pieces and removed before the problem of the sarcophagus could be contemplated. Thus we labored for another month, first dismantling the second shrine, then the third, until the fourth was completely freed. When this was achieved we saw that this last shrine had all the appearance of a golden tabernacle. Upon its folding doors and west end were winged figures of the goddesses of the dead, in fine bas-relief, majestic in their protective significance, while the walls of the shrine were covered with religious texts.

We found between the third and fourth innermost shrines ceremonial bows and arrows, and with them, a pair of the gorgeous fans prominent in scenes where kings are depicted. They were beautiful specimens, one lying at the head, the other along the south side of the innermost shrine. The one at the head, in sheet gold, bore a charming historical scene of the young Tut-ankh-Amen in his chariot, followed by his favorite hound, hunting ostriches for feathers for the fan; on the reverse side of the fan, also finely embossed and chased, the young "Lord of Valor" is depicted returning triumphant, his quarry, two ostriches, borne on the shoulders of two attendants who precede him, the plumes under his arm. The second fan, larger and perhaps more resplendent, was of ebony overlaid with sheet gold and encrusted with turquoise, lapis lazuli, and carnelian-colored glass, as well as translucent calcite: the palm of the fan was emblazoned with the title of Tut-ankh-Amen. Only the debris remained of the feathers of these two fans. Although these had suffered from the havoc of insects, enough still remained to show us that there had been alternate white and brown plumes—forty-two on each fan.

The roof and cornice of the fourth innermost shrine, contrary to our expectations, was of different form, and was made in one piece instead of in several sections. It was thus very heavy, and it took several laborious days before it could be lifted, gradually turned, and hauled into the Antechamber. Taking apart the sides, ends, and doors of this innermost shrine was a much easier undertaking. It enclosed and, as it proved, exactly fitted the sarcophagus. Our task of over eighty days was thus ended.

During the process of our work it became clear that the ancient Egyptian undertakers must have had extreme difficulty in erecting the shrines within

Raising the lid of the innermost shrine

that limited space. It must have been necessary for them first to have placed the parts of the four shrines in correct order around the four walls of the chamber. The carpentry and joining of those constructions exhibited great skill, and each section was carefully numbered and oriented to show not only how they fitted, but also their correct orientation. The constructors of those shrines were past masters in their work, but there was evidence that the obsequies had been hurriedly performed, and that the workmen in charge of those last rites were anything but careful men. They had leaned the parts of the shrines against the four walls around the sarcophagus contrary to instructions, so when the shrines were erected, the doors faced east instead of west,

The sarcophagus when first freed of the four covering shrines

the foot ends west instead of east, and the side panels were likewise transposed. This may have been a pardonable fault, the chamber being too small for correct orientation, but there were other signs of slovenliness. Sections had obviously been banged together, regardless of the risk of damage to their gilt ornamentation. Deep dents from blows from a heavy hammerlike implement were visible on the gold work, in some cases parts of the surfaces had been knocked off, and the workmen's refuse, such as chips of wood, had never been cleared away.

With the raising of the roof and the removal of the three sides and doors of the fourth shrine stood the magnificent sarcophagus of wonderful workmanship, carved out of a solid block of finest yellow quartzite, nine feet long, four feet ten inches wide, and four feet ten inches high.

It was on February 3rd that we first saw clearly this sepulchral masterpiece,

The sarcophagus—the goddess Selkit carved in high relief

96

ranking among the finest specimens of its kind. The outstanding features of the sarcophagus were the guardian goddesses Isis, Nephthys, Neith, and Selkit, carved in high relief on each of the four corners, so placed that their full spread wings and outstretched arms encircle the coffin with their protective embrace. Around the base are protective symbols *Ded* and *Thet*. The corners of the casket rested upon alabaster slabs. Between the last shrine and the sarcophagus there were no objects, save for a *Ded*-symbol placed on the south side for strength and possibly protection of the owner.

As our light fell on the noble quartzite monument it illuminated, in repeated

The outermost (first) coffin within the sarcophagus

detail, that last solemn appeal to gods and men, and made us feel that, in the young king's case, a dignity had been added even to death. With the profound silence that reigned, emotion deepened, the past and present seemed to meet —we asked ourselves: was it not yesterday that, with pomp and ceremony, they had laid the young king in that casket?—so fresh, so seemingly recent, were those touching claims on our pity that, the more we gazed on them, the more the illusion gathered strength. It made us wish that Tut-ankh-Amen's journey through the underworld might be unperturbed until he attained complete bliss, as those four goddesses, sculptured in high relief at the corners, seemed to plead as they shielded their charge.

The lid, made of rose granite tinted to match the sarcophagus, was cracked in the middle and firmly embedded in the covered up edges. The cracks had been carefully cemented and painted over to match the rest, in such a way as to leave no doubt that it had not been tampered with.

Undoubtedly the original intention must have been to provide a quartzite lid in keeping with the sarcophagus itself; some accident must have occurred. It may be that the intended lid was not ready in time for the burial of the king, and that this crudely made granite slab was substituted.

The crack greatly complicated the raising of this lid, for had it been intact the operation would have been far easier. However, the difficulty was overcome by passing angle irons along and closely fitting the sides of the slab, which permitted it to be raised by pulleys in one piece.

We had now reached the supreme culminating moment—a moment we had looked forward to ever since it became evident that the chambers discovered, in November, 1922, must be the tomb of Tut-ankh-Amen, and not a cache of his furniture. All of us were affected by the prospect of what we were about to see—the burial custom of a king of ancient Egypt of thirty-three centuries ago. How would the king be found?

The tackle for raising the lid was in position. I gave the word. Amid intense silence the huge slab, broken in two, weighing over a ton and a quarter, rose from its bed. The light shone into the sarcophagus. A sight met our eyes that at first puzzled and disappointed us. The contents were completely covered by fine linen shrouds. We rolled back these shrouds, one by one, and as the last was removed a gasp of wonderment escaped our lips, so gorgeous was the sight that met our eye: a golden effigy of the young boy king, of most magnificent workmanship, filled the whole of the interior of the sarcophagus. This

The head of the effigy upon the first coffin

was the lid of a wonderful coffin in the form of the young king, some seven feet in length, resting upon a low bier in the form of a lion, and no doubt the outermost in a series of coffins, nested one within the other, enclosing the mortal remains of the king. Clasping the body of this magnificent monument were two winged goddesses. Isis and Neith, wrought in rich goldwork upon gesso, as brilliant as the day the coffin was made. While this decoration was rendered in fine bas-relief, the head and hands of the king were in the round, in massive gold of the finest sculpture, surpassing anything we could have imagined. The hands, crossed over the breast, held the royal emblems—the Crook and the Flail—encrusted with deep blue faience. The face and features were wonderfully wrought in sheet gold. The eyes were of aragonite and obsidian, the eyebrows and eyelids inlaid with lapis lazuli. There was a touch of realism, for while the rest of this coffin, covered with feathered ornament, was of brilliant gold, that of the bare face and hands seemed different, the gold of the flesh being of different alloy, thus conveying an impression of the grayness of death. Upon the forehead of this recumbent figure of the king were two emblems delicately worked in brilliant inlay—the Cobra and the Vulture—symbols of upper and lower Egypt, but perhaps the most touching, in its human simplicity, was the tiny wreath of flowers around these symbols, as it pleased us to think, the last farewell offering of the widowed girl queen to her husband, the youthful representative of the "Two Kingdoms."

Those few withered flowers, still retaining their tinge of color, told us what a short period 3,300 years really was—but yesterday and tomorrow.

Thus from stairway, steep descending passage, Antechamber and Burial Chamber, from those golden shrines and from that noble sarcophagus, our eyes were now turned to its contents—a gold-encased coffin, in form a recumbent figure of the young king, symbolizing Osiris, or, it would seem, by its fearless gaze, man's ancient trust in immortality. Many and disturbing were the emotions awakened in us. In that silence, you could almost hear the ghostly footsteps of the departing mourners.

Our lights were lowered, once more we mounted those sixteen steps, once more we beheld the blue vault of the heavens, where the sun is lord, but our inner thoughts still lingered over the splendor of the vanished pharaoh, with his last appeal upon his coffin written upon our minds: "Oh Mother Nût! spread thy wings over me as the Imperishable Stars."

Opening the Three Coffins

On October 10, 1925, at 6:30 A.M. the uncovering of the entrance of the tomb commenced. The men and boys eagerly set to work to remove the mass of rubbish heaped over the entrance staircase for protective purposes at the end of the previous season's work. They labored like ants, and although the temperature in the Valley was ranging from 97° to 105°, and the air gray with dust, they worked enthusiastically.

The clearance of the entrance to the tomb was finished on the following day, when we were able to connect up our electrical installation with that of the Royal Tombs, and inspect the interior.

Familiarity can never entirely dissipate the feeling of mystery—the sense of vanished but haunting forces—that clings to the tomb. The conviction of the unity of past and present is constantly impressed upon the archaeological adventurer, even when absorbed in the mechanical details of his work.

And now once more our powerful electric lamps lit up the great quartzite sarcophagus. Under the plate glass screen which I had placed over it was revealed the gold-encased coffin.

The task before us then was to raise the lid of the first outermost coffin as it rested in the sarcophagus.

After careful study of the coffin we decided that the original silver handles —two on each side—were sufficiently well preserved to support the weight of the lid and could be used without danger in raising it. The lid was fixed to the shell by means of ten solid silver tongues, fitted into corresponding sockets in the shell, where they were held in place by substantial gold-headed silver pins. Could we remove the silver pins by which the lid was fixed to the shell of the coffin without disturbing the coffin in the sarcophagus? As the coffin filled up nearly the whole of the interior of the sarcophagus, it was by no means easy to extract the pins. By careful manipulation, however, it was found possible to withdraw them, except for the pin at the head end where there was only space enough to pull it half out. It had to be filed through before the inner half could be withdrawn.

The next step was to place in position the hoisting tackle necessary for lifting the lid. The tackle was attached to the handles of the lid of the coffin by means of slings, thus assuring a correct centralization of its weight, otherwise there would have been a danger of the lid bumping against the sides of the sarcophagus.

It was a moment as anxious as exciting. The lid came up fairly readily, revealing a second magnificent anthropoid coffin, covered with a thin gossamer linen sheet, darkened and much decayed. Upon this linen shroud were lying floral garlands, composed of olive and willow leaves, petals of the blue lotus, and cornflowers, while a small wreath of similar kind had been placed, also over the shroud, on the emblems of the forehead. Underneath this covering were rich multicolored glass decoration encrusted upon the fine goldwork of the coffin.

This undertaking was completed in one morning. The tomb was then closed and everything left undisturbed to await Harry Burton's photographic records.

Thus far our progress had been fairly satisfactory, but we now became conscious of a rather ominous feature. The second coffin showed distinct signs of the effect of some form of dampness and, here and there, tendency for its beautiful inlay to fall away. This was disconcerting, suggesting as it did the existence of former humidity of some kind within the nest of coffins. Should this prove the case, the preservation of the royal mummy would be less satisfactory than we had hoped.

On October 15, Mr. Burton arrived, and on the 17th, he successfully completed the photographic records of the shroud and floral garlands that covered the second coffin as it rested within the shell of the first, in the sarcophagus.

We had to consider how to deal with the second coffin, as well as the shell of the first. Our difficulties were increased on account of the depth of the sarcophagus, and it was evident that the outer shell and the second coffin, neither of which was in a condition to bear much handling, must be raised together. This was eventually accomplished by means of pulleys attached by steel pins passed through the tongue sockets of the first outermost shell. In this way hoisting was possible with a minimum of handling.

In spite of the great weight of the coffins they were successfully raised to just above the level of the top of the sarcophagus, and wooden planks were passed under them. In the confined space and with the restricted headroom available, the task proved difficult. It was much increased by the necessity of avoiding damage to the fragile gesso-gilt surfaces of the outermost coffin.

Further records having been taken, I was able to remove the chaplet and garlands, and roll back the covering shroud. We could now gaze, with admiring eyes, upon the finest example of the ancient coffin-maker's art ever yet seen, most delicate in conception, and very beautiful in line. As it lay in the outer shell which rested upon the modern improvised trestles, it presented a wonderful picture of Majesty lying in State.

This second coffin, six feet eight inches long, sumptuously inlaid on thick gold foil with cut and engraved opaque glass, simulating red jasper, lapis lazuli, and turquoise, was similar in form and design to the first. It symbolizes Osiris in ornament, but it differs in certain detail. In this case the king wears the *Nemses* headdress and the body is embraced by the vulture, Nekhebet, and the serpent, Buto. The arresting feature is the delicacy and superiority of the conception, which confer upon it at once the position of a masterpiece.

We were now faced by a complicated problem. Seeing that there were handles on the outer coffin for lowering or raising the lid, we expected similar metal handles on the second coffin. There were none, and their absence placed us in a dilemma. The second coffin proved exceedingly heavy; its decorated surface very fragile. It fitted the outer shell so closely that it was not possible to pass one's little finger between the two. Its lid was fixed, as in the case of the outer coffin, with gold-headed silver pins which, as the coffin lay in the outer shell, could not be extracted. It would have to be lifted in its entirety from the outer shell before anything further could be done.

Howard Carter working on the second coffin

Removing the second coffin from the outermost (first) coffin

We could not be sure that the wood of the coffin was sufficiently well preserved to bear its own weight. However, after long consultations and having studied the problem for nearly two days, we devised a plan. To remove the second coffin from the shell of the first, some points of attachment were necessary. It was judged best to make use of the metal pins which fastened down the lid.

Inspection showed that although the space between the shell of the outer coffin and the second coffin was insufficient to enable us to withdraw these pins entirely, they could still be pulled out about a quarter of an inch, so as to permit stout copper wire attachments to be fixed to them and to the overhead scaffold. This we did successfully. Strong metal eyelets were then screwed into the top edge of the shell of the outer coffin, so as to enable it to be lowered from the second coffin by means of ropes working on the pulleys.

On the following day we were able to proceed with the next stage. It proved to be one of the most important moments in the dismantling of the tomb. The process adopted was the reverse of that which might appear to be natural. We lowered the outer shell from the second coffin, instead of lifting the second coffin out of the first, because the headroom was insufficient, and the weight being stationary, there would be less risk of undue stress upon those ancient silver pins. The shell of the outer coffin was lowered once more into the sarcophagus, leaving, for a moment, the second coffin suspended in midair by means of the ten stout wire attachments. A wooden tray sufficiently large to span the opening of the sarcophagus was then passed under it, and the second coffin, strongly supported, stood before us free and accessible. The wire attachments having been severed and the overhead gear removed, Mr. Burton made his record, and we were able to turn our energies to the raising of its lid.

The entire inlaid surface was indeed in a very fragile condition, and any handling had to be avoided. In order to lift the lid without causing injury, metal eyelets, to serve as handles, were screwed into it at four points where there would be no danger of permanent disfigurement. To these eyelets our hoisting tackle was fixed, the gold-headed silver nails were extracted, and the lid was slowly raised.

There was some slight tendency for the lid to stick, but gradually it rose from its bed and, when high enough to clear the contents of the coffin, it was lowered onto a wooden tray.

This revealed a third coffin, also, Osiride in form, but the main details of the workmanship were hidden by a close-fitting reddish-colored linen shroud. The burnished gold face was bare; placed over the neck and breast was an elaborate bead and floral collarette, sewn upon a backing of papyrus, and tucked immediately above the Nemses headdress was a linen napkin.

Mr. Burton at once took his photographs. I then removed the floral collarette and linen coverings. An astounding fact was disclosed: this third coffin, six feet, one-and-three-quarters inches long, was solid gold! The mystery of the enormous weight, which had puzzled us, was now clear. It explained also why the weight had diminished so slightly after the first coffin, and the lid of the second coffin, had been removed. Its weight was still as much as eight strong men could lift.

The face of this gold coffin was again that of the king, but the features though conventional, by symbolizing Osiris, were even more youthful than those on the other coffins. In actual design it reverted to that of the outermost coffin and had engraved upon it figures of Isis and Nephthys, but auxiliary to this design were winged figures of Nekhebet and Buto. These latter protective figures, emblematic of upper and lower Egypt, were the prominent feature, for they were superimposed in gorgeous and massive cloisonné work over the richly engraved ornament of the coffin—their inlay being natural semiprecious stones. In addition to this decoration, over the conventional collarette of "the Hawk"—again in auxiliary cloisonné work—was a double detachable necklace of large disk-shaped beads of red and yellow gold and blue faience, which enhanced the richness of the whole effect. But the ultimate details of the ornamentation were hidden by a black lustrous coating due to liquid unguents that had evidently been profusely poured over the coffin. As a result this unparalleled monument was not only disfigured—only temporarily, as it afterward proved—but was stuck fast to the interior of the second coffin, the consolidated liquid filling up the space between the second and third coffins almost to the level of the lid of the third.

These consecration unguents, which had obviously been used in great quantity, were doubtless the cause of the disintegration observed when dealing with the outer coffins which, as they were in a practically hermetically sealed quartzite sarcophagus, cannot have been affected by outside influences. The covering shroud and floral collarette mingled with blue faience beads had also suffered, and although these at first appeared to be in good condition, they

Howard Carter working on the third coffin

proved so brittle that the material broke the very instant it was touched.

We raised the third coffin contained in the shell of the second, which now rested on the top of the sarcophagus, and moved them into the Antechamber where they were more accessible, both for examination and manipulation. It was then that the wonder and magnitude of our last discovery more completely dawned upon us. This unique and wonderful monument—a coffin over six feet in length, of the finest art, wrought in solid gold about one-tenth of an inch thick—represented an enormous mass of pure bullion.

How great must have been the wealth buried with those ancient pharaohs! What riches that valley must have once concealed! Of the twenty-seven monarchs buried there, Tut-ankh-Amen was probably of the least importance. How great must have been the temptation to the greed and rapacity of the audacious contemporary tomb robbers! What stronger incentive can be imagined than those vast treasures of gold! The plundering of royal tombs becomes easily intelligible when the incentive to these crimes is measured by this gold coffin of Tut-ankh-Amen. It must have represented fabulous wealth to the stonecutters, artisans, water-carriers and peasants—to contemporary workers generally, such as the men implicated in the tomb robberies.

Our object now was to protect from injury and to conserve the delicate inlay on the shell of the second coffin. Therefore it was lightly brushed to remove loose dust, sponged with warm water and ammonia, and, when dry, the whole surface covered with a thick coating of paraffin wax applied hot with a long brush. This wax as it cooled and solidified held the inlay securely in position so that the coffin could be handled with impunity.

We then had to experiment to ascertain the most satisfactory and at the same time the quickest manner of dealing with those ancient consecration unguents that not only covered the body of the coffin but completely filled the space between the two, thus sticking them fast and for the moment preventing further progress. This substance was black and resembled pitch; where the layer was thin it was hard and brittle, but where a thicker layer had accumulated, the interior of the material was soft and plastic. When warm it smelled somewhat fragrant, not unpleasant, and suggestive of wood pitch. There can be no doubt from the manner in which this material had run down the sides of the third coffin and connected underneath, that it was in a liquid or semiliquid condition when it was employed.

It follows that this substance could be melted by heat and dissolved by

The innermost (third) coffin which contained the mummy

certain solvents, but neither of these methods was practicable. So we decided to raise the lid of the third coffin and examine the contents before applying any drastic measures. Luckily the line of junction between the lid and the coffin was visible and, with difficulty, accessible, except at the extreme foot end where the second and third coffins practically touched.

The lid was fastened to the shell by means of eight gold tenons (four on each side), which were held in their sockets by nails. Thus if the nails could be extracted the lid could be raised. In the narrow space between the two coffins ordinary implements for extracting metal pins were useless, and others, had to be devised. With long screwdrivers converted to meet the conditions, the solid gold nails were removed piecemeal. The lid was raised by its golden handles and the mummy of the king disclosed.

Three thousand years and more had elapsed since men's eyes had gazed into that golden coffin. Here at last lay all that was left of the youthful pharaoh, hitherto little more to us than the shadow of a name.

Occupying the entire interior of the golden coffin was an impressive, neat, and carefully made mummy, over which had been poured anointing unguents, as in the case of the outside of its coffin, again in great quantity, consolidated and blackened by age. In contrast to the general dark and somber effect, due to these unguents, was a brilliant, magnificent, burnished gold mask of the king, covered his head and shoulders, which, like the feet, had been intentionally avoided when using the unguents. The mummy was fashioned to symbolize Osiris. The beaten gold mask, a beautiful and unique specimen of ancient portraiture, bears a sad but calm expression suggestive of youth overtaken prematurely by death. Upon its forehead, wrought in massive gold, were the royal insignia—the Nekhebet Vulture and Buto Serpent, emblems of the Two Kingdoms over which he had reigned. To the chin was attached the conventional Osiride beard, wrought in gold and lapis-lazuli-colored glass; around the throat was a triple necklace of yellow and red gold and blue faience disk-shaped beads; pendant from the neck by flexible gold inlaid straps was a large black resin scarab that rested between the hands. The burnished gold hands, crossed over the breast, separate from the mask, were sewn to the material of the linen wrappings, and grasped the Flagellum and Crozier—the emblems of Osiris. Immediately below these was the simple outermost linen covering, adorned with richly inlaid gold trappings pendant from a large pectoral-like figure of the *Ba* bird or soul, of gold cloisonné work, its full-

Tut-ankh-Amen's gold mummy mask

256

A

spread wings stretched over the body. As these gorgeous trappings had been subjected to the consecration unguents, their detail and brilliance were hardly visible, and to this must be attributed the disastrous deterioration which we discovered to have taken place in the case of many of the objects.

But through this obstruction it could be faintly seen that these trappings, made of heavy gold plaques held together by threads of beads, bore welcoming speeches of the gods—for example, on the longitudinal bands down the center, the goddess of the sky, Nût, the Divine Mother, says: "I reckon thy beauties, O Osiris, King Kheperu-neb-Re; thy soul livest: thy veins are firm. Thou smellest the air and goest out as a god, going out as Atum, O Osiris, Tut-ankh-Amen. Thou goest out and thou enterest with Ra . . ." The god of the earth, the prince of the gods, Geb, says: "My beloved son, inheritor of the throne of Osiris, the King Kheperu-neb-Re; thy nobility is perfect: thy Royal Palace is powerful; thy name is in the mouth of the Rekhyt, thy stability is in the mouth of the living, O Osiris, King Tut-ankh-Amen, thy heart is in thy body, like Re he rests in heaven." The texts upon the transverse bands open with words such as "Honored before Anubis, Hepy, Qebeh-sne wef, Dua-mutef," and "Justified before Osiris."

When these trappings were cleaned it became clear that the jeweler had made the main part (texts and festoons) to measure, that the finished mummy proved larger than was originally expected, and that pieces were cut, others added, to make them fit.

Those liquid unguents would seem to have been applied as part of the burial ritual for the consecration of the dead king, before his entrance into the presence of the great god Osiris of the underworld.

When the detailed photographs had been made by Mr. Burton, we were better able to examine closely the actual state of preservation of the mummy. The greater part of the flagellum and crozier was completely decomposed, and had already fallen to dust; the threads that once held the hands and trappings in place upon the outer linen covering were decayed, and in consequence the various sections fell apart at the slightest touch; the black resin scarab was covered by minute fissures, probably the result of contraction; consequently, these external trappings and ornaments had to be removed, piece by piece, and placed in corresponding order and position upon a tray for future cleaning and remounting. The farther we proceeded the more evident it became that the covering wrappings and the mummy were both in a perilous state.

They were completely carbonized by the action that had been set up by the fatty acids of the unguents with which they had been saturated.

But alas! Both the mask and the mummy were stuck fast to the bottom of the coffin by the consolidated residue of the unguents, and no amount of legitimate force could move them. What was to be done?

Since it was known that this adhesive material could be softened by.heat, it was hoped that an exposure to the midday sun would melt it sufficiently to allow the mummy to be raised. A trial was made for several hours in sun temperature reaching as high as 149°, without any success and, as other means were not practicable, it became evident that we should have to make all further examination of the king's remains as they lay within the two coffins.

After the scientific examination of the king's mummy *in situ,* and its final removal from the gold coffin, the very difficult question of removing the gold mask and extricating the gold coffin from the shell of the second coffin had to be solved.

Originally something like two bucketfuls of the liquid unguents had been poured over the golden coffin, and a similar amount over the body inside. As heat was the only practicable means of melting this material and rendering it malleable, in order to apply a temperature sufficiently high for the purpose, without causing damage to those wonderful specimens of ancient Egyptian art, the interior of the golden coffin had to be completely lined with thick plates of zinc which would not melt under a temperature of 968°. The coffins were then placed upside down on trestles, the outside one being protected against undue heat and fire by several blankets saturated and kept wet with water. Our next procedure was to place under the hollow of the gold coffin several paraffin lamps burning at full blast. The heat from the lamps had to be regulated so as to keep the temperature well within the melting point of zinc. It should be noted here that the coating of wax upon the surface of the second coffin acted as a pyrometer—while it remained unmelted under the wet blanketing there was clearly no fear of injury.

Although the temperature arrived at was some 932°, it took several hours before any real effect was noticeable. The moment signs of movement became apparent the lamps were turned out, and the coffins left suspended upon the trestles, when after an hour, they began to fall apart. The movement at first was almost imperceptible owing to the tenacity of the material, but we were able to separate them by lifting up the wooden shell of the second coffin, thus leaving the shell of the gold coffin resting upon the trestles. Its very nature was hardly recognizable, and all we could see was a dripping mass of viscous pitchlike material which proved very difficult to remove, even with quantities of various solvents.

The interior was also covered with a viscid mass, to which the gold mask still adhered. This mask had been protected by being bound with a folded wet blanket continually fed with water, its face padded with wet wadding. As it had been subjected to the full power of the heat collected in the interior of the coffin, it was freed and lifted away with comparative ease, although a great mass of viscous unguents adhered to its back, which had to be removed with the aid of a blast lamp and cleaning solvents.

We then returned to the first coffin, that had to be raised out of the sarcophagus. This was successfully achieved by means of our hoisting tackle attached to the overhead scaffolding. After it was high enough to clear the top of the sarcophagus, a wooden tray was passed beneath it, and it was thus carried up to the laboratory, where its lid was already under treatment. It proved to be of great weight, and, like the shrines, was probably of oak. It had unfortunately suffered from humidity evaporated from those liquid unguents, which had caused the gesso-gilt surfaces to blister and buckle to such an extent that, in many places, this overlaying decoration had become detached from the basic wood. By our patiently filling in the interstices with hot paraffin wax, in time, with care, it was repaired, and the decorated surfaces once more made good and firm.

The only remaining object in the sarcophagus was the gilt bed-shaped bier with lion's head and feet. It stood on the bottom and served as a support to the first (outermost) coffin. It was made of a stout and heavy wood covered with gesso-gilt; but the astonishing fact was that after supporting the weight—more than a ton and a quarter—of those three great coffins for over thirty centuries, it was still intact. Strips of broad webbing were passed under it, and this splendid example of ancient Egyptian construction was raised out of the sarcophagus. It stood about twelve inches high, seven feet six inches long, and was curved so as to receive and to fit the base of the outermost coffin. The central panel was designed in low relief to represent a cord-mesh. The joints of the framework were hardly sprung, thus bearing witness to the good quality of the wood and the extreme excellence of the joinery.

Lying on the bottom of the sarcophagus beneath this bier were a number of wooden chips bearing traces of gesso-gilt ornamentation. The design on the gesso-gilt surface was identical with that on the edge of the first coffin, from which pieces had been crudely hacked away by some sharp instrument like a carpenter's adze. The foot end of the coffin, as it rested on the bier, must have been too high to allow the lid of the sarcophagus to be lowered in place, and it was therefore cut down by those whose duty it was to close the sarcophagus. This is evidence of want of forethought on the part of the workmen. This mutilation of the coffin had not been noticed before, owing to its having been hidden by the anointing unguents.

The Burial Chamber and sarcophagus were now empty and we were able, for the first time, to consider more closely the funerary customs followed in the burial of a pharaoh, as revealed to us by Tut-ankh-Amen's tomb.

The more we considered it the more we were impressed by the extreme care and enormous costliness lavished by this ancient people on the enshrinement of their dead. Barrier after barrier was raised to guard their remains from the predatory hands against which, in death, these great kings so ineffectually sought protection. The process was as elaborate as it was costly.

Examination of
the Royal Mummy

To most investigators, and especially to those absorbed in archaeological research, there are moments when their work becomes of transcending interest, and it was now our good fortune to pass through one of these rare and wonderful periods. After years of toil of excavating, conserving and recording, we were to see with the eye of reality that which we had hitherto beheld only in imagination.

On November 11, 1925, at 9:45 A.M., the examination of the royal mummy commenced.

The external ornaments and inlaid gold trappings have been removed, the king's mummy lay bare with its simple outer coverings and gold mask. It occupied the whole of the interior of the gold coffin, measuring in total length six feet, one inch.

Because of the fragile and carbonized condition of the linen swathing, the exposed surface was painted over with melted paraffin wax. When it congealed, it formed a thin coating on the surface, with minimum penetration of the decayed wrappings beneath. When the wax had cooled, Dr. Douglas Derry made a longitudinal incision down the center of the outer binding to the depth penetrated by the wax, thus enabling the consolidated layer to be removed in large pieces. Nor did our troubles end here. The voluminous underwrappings were found to be in even worse condition of carbonization and decay. We had hoped, by removing a thin outer layer of bandage from the mummy, to free it so that it might be removed, but we were again disappointed. It was found that the linen beneath the mummy and the body itself were so saturated in the unguents which formed a pitchlike mass at the bottom of the coffin and held it embedded so firmly, that it was impossible to raise it except at the risk of great damage. Even after most of the bandages had been carefully removed, the consolidated material had to be chiseled away from beneath the limbs and trunk before it was possible to raise the king's remains.

The bandages that acutally enveloped the head were in a better state of preservation than those on the body. They had not been saturated by the unguents, and consequently had only suffered from indirect oxidation. This was also the case to a large extent with the wrappings on the feet.

The general system of bandaging so far as could be discovered was of normal character: it comprised a series of bandages, sheets, and pads of linen, where the latter were required to complete the anthropoid form, the whole showing evidence of considerable care. The linen was very fine. The numerous objects found upon the mummy were caught up in many different layers of bindings which were wound crosswise and transversely.

The removal of the final wrappings that protected the face of the king needed the utmost care, as owing to the carbonized state of the head there was always the risk of injury to the fragile features. At the touch of a sable brush the last few fragments of decayed fabric fell away, revealing a serene and placid countenance, that of a young man. The face was refined and cultured, the features well formed, especially the clearly marked lips, and the first and most striking impression of all present was the remarkable structural resemblance to his father-in-law, Akh-en-Aten—an affinity that had been visible on the monuments.

There is one more point of great interest. The king's head shows that the finer contemporary representations of him upon the monuments beyond all doubt, are accurate portraits of Tut-ankh-Amen.

Upon the king's neck there were two kinds of symbolical collars and twenty amulets grouped in six layers; and between each of these layers were numerous linen bandages.

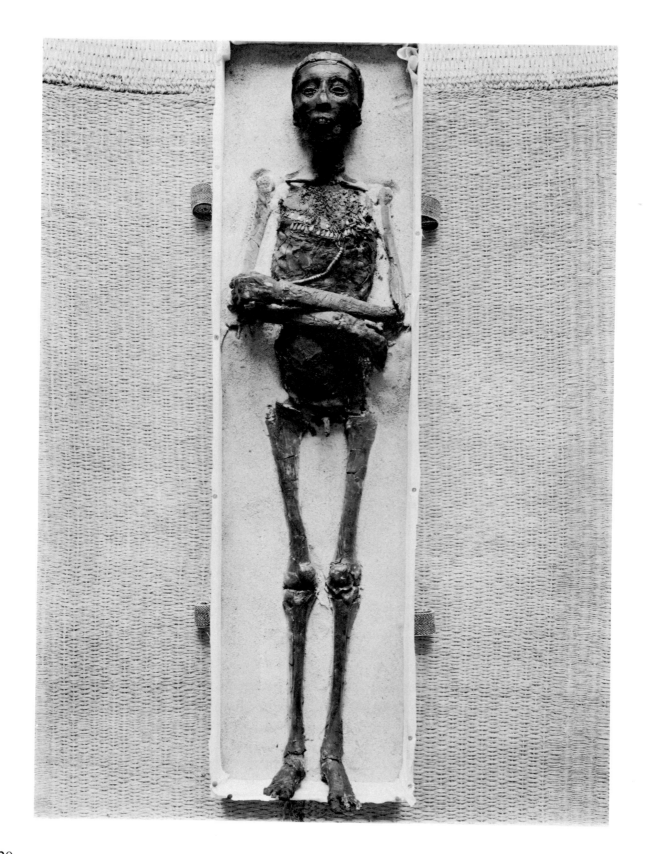

This profusion of amulets and sacred symbols placed on the neck of the king are extremely significant, suggesting as they do how greatly the dangers of the underworld were feared for the dead. No doubt they were intended to protect him against injury on his journey through the hereafter. The quality and quantity of these protective symbols would naturally depend on his high rank and wealth, as well as upon the affection of his survivors. The actual meaning of many of them is not clear, nor do we know the exact nomenclature, nor the powers ascribed to them. However, we do know that they were placed there for the help and guidance of the dead, and made as beautiful and costly as possible.

In accordance with the Book of the Dead, whoever wears the *Ded*—the emblem of Osiris—may "enter into the realms of the dead, eat the food of Osiris, and be justified." He on whom the *Thet* symbol—the girdle of Isis—is hung, will be guarded by Isis and Horus, and be welcomed with joy into the Kingdom of Osiris.

We learn also from the Book of the Dead that when these mystic emblems were placed on the deceased, the magic spells associated with them were to be uttered "in solemn voice." In the case of the amulets and symbols found upon the king, there were traces of a small papyrus that bore a ritual, written in white linear hieroglyphs, but too decayed and disintegrated to allow practical conservation, though here and there names of gods, such as Osiris and Isis, were with difficulty decipherable. This diminutive document, disintegrated beyond recovery, possibly pertained to such spells.

The royal mummy

The Treasury Beyond the Burial Chamber

We next directed our energies toward the Storeroom beyond the Burial Chamber, perhaps better named "The Innermost Treasury."

This room is not more than fifteen feet eight inches long, by twelve feet six inches square, and seven feet eight inches in height. Entrance is by means of a low open doorway cut in the northern end of the west wall of the Burial Chamber. It is of extreme simplicity, there being no attempt at decoration. The four walls and ceiling were unsmoothed, the marks of the final chiseling still visible upon the rock surfaces. In fact, it is just as those ancient Egyptian masons left it—even the last few flakes of limestone from their chisels lay on the floor.

Small and simple as it is, the impressive memories of the past haunt it none the less. When one entered such a room as this for the first time, the sanctity of which had been inviolate for more than thirty centuries, a sense of reverence, if not of fear, is felt. It seemed almost desecration to trouble that long peace and to break that eternal silence. One hesitates before venturing to enter and explore, until remembering that, however much one may respect the past, an archaeologist's duty is to the present. It is for him to interpret what is hidden.

The doorway of this room, unlike the others, was not bricked up or sealed; from it we had a clear view of the contents. Within a few days of its discovery (February 17, 1923), after briefly surveying its contents, we purposely closed the doorway with wooden boards, so as not to be distracted or tempted to disturb any of the objects in this little room while dealing with the material in the Burial Chamber. In early 1927 we removed that wooden boarding, and after four years' patient waiting, our attention was once more directed within. All it held was again revealed—objects both of mystic and of absorbing interest, but mostly of purely funerary nature and of intense religious character.

Unquestionably the thieves had entered this little room, but in their predatory quest they seem to have done little harm other than to open and rifle the treasure caskets and some boxes. At first sight, the only visible evidence of their visit were some beads and tiny fragments of jewelery scattered on the floor, the broken seals and displaced lids of caskets, folds of linen hanging from the mouths of the boxes, and here and there an overturned object. The robbers must have been aware of the nature of the contents of this room for, with rare exception, only those boxes which held objects of intrinsic value had been disturbed.

Among the heterogeneous collection of objects we find the Canopic equipment safeguards for the deceased's passage through the Underworld; and objects that the deceased required for his use in daily life, and hence would continue to require in his future life: jewelery for his adornment, chariots for his recreation, and servants (*Shawabti*-figures) to carry out any irksome work he might be called upon to do in the hereafter. Housed in black shrinelike chests were statuettes representing the king in the act of divine pursuit and figures of the gods, to help him through the dangers to which he might be exposed. There were boats to render the deceased independent of the favors of the "celestial ferrymen," or to enable him to follow Re, the Sun-god, on his nocturnal voyage through the interconnecting tunnels of the Underworld and in his triumphal journey across the heavens. There were also barques, fully rigged and equipped with cabins, symbolizing the funeral pilgrimage; there was a granary filled with grain; a saddle-stone for grinding corn; strainers for the preparation of beer; and there was even a mock figure representing the regermination of Osiris, the revered god of the dead, who, like man, suffered death, was buried, and afterward rose again to immortal life.

The Funerary Equipment

A firm conviction among the ancient Egyptians was that life did not end at death, but that man continued to live just as he had lived upon this earth, provided that measures for his protection to usher him through the labyrinth of the underworld and necessities for his future existence were assured him.

The figure of the god Anubis, who takes upon himself the form of a kind of black jackal-like dog without gender, who not only presided over the burial rites but also acted as the vigilant watcher over the dead, was appropriately placed in the open doorway, facing outward toward the west. It enabled him to watch over the Burial Chamber and its occupant while he also guarded his domain the "Treasure of the Innermost."

The magical torch and clay-brick pedestal found at the entrance of this room, with its tiny reed torch and a few grains of charcoal, seem not to have been dropped by mere chance on the floor within the threshold in front of Anubis. The magical formula scratched upon the brick tells us: "It is I who hinder the sand from choking the secret chamber. I am for the protection of the Osiris (the deceased)."

To depart for a moment from the main subject; what was the origin of this very interesting Anubis animal? The majority of the animal's characteristics are those of the domestic dog, but in place of the curved tail peculiar to the dog, it has the long, straight tail of the fox, clublike in form, which it carried in drooping position like the wolf, jackal, or fox. The numerous representations of this Anubis animal upon the Egyptian monuments resemble largely the bearing of the jackal, and it may have been a domesticated form of the jackal crossed with another subgenus of the canine family. The collar and the scarflike leash that are invariably represented round its neck also suggest an animal brought under human control. And when one takes into account the qualities of the domesticated canine—devotion to his master, knowledge and defense of his property, attachment to him until death—it may explain why those ancients selected this jackal-like dog as the vigilant watcher over their dead.

Characteristics of the Anubis beast are often very noticeable among a black species of the native Egyptian dogs, but like all the Egyptian pariahs they have a curled tail, coiled tightly over the rump, and never straight and drooping like that of the Anubis.

The fact that this animal is invariably represented genderless suggests the possibility of its being an imaginary beast.

The Canopic equipment stood before the center of the east end wall immediately opposite the entrance doorway. It was six feet six inches in height, and it occupied a floor area of some five by four feet. The monument's simple grandeur, and the calm which seemed to accompany the four little gracious statuettes that guarded it, produced a mystery and an appeal to the imagination that would be difficult to describe.

The shielding canopy overlaid with gold was supported by four corner posts upon a massive sledge, its cornice surmounted with brilliantly inlaid solar cobras; on each side was a lifelike gilded satutette of a tutelary goddess, guarding her charge with outstretched protective arms. The central portion— a large shrine-shaped chest—also completely overlaid with gold and surmounted with solar cobras, concealed a smaller chest hewn out of a solid block of veined semitranslucent alabaster (calcite). This alabaster chest, with gilt dado, covered with a linen pall, standing upon a silver-handled gesso-gilt wooden sledge, held the four receptacles for the internal organs of the king. The organs, wrapped in separate mummiform packages, were in four miniature gold coffins.

In the Egyptian process of mummifying the body, the internal organs were

The god Anubis

The Canopic chest open showing the four human-headed lids

separately preserved in four receptacles and charged to the genii Imsety, Hepy, Dua-mutef, and Qebeh-sne wef, who were under the special protection of the goddesses Isis, Nepthys, Neith, and Selkit. Each of these four tutelary goddesses was supposed to have possesed within herself a genius, which it was her duty to protect. An ancient myth connected with the four genii, said to be the sons of Horus, tells us that they arose from water in a lily, and that the crocodile god, Sebekh, commanded by the sun god, Re, had to catch them in a net. However, it is also said that Isis produced them, and that they succored Osiris in his misfortunes, and saved him from hunger and thirst, and hence it became their office to do the same for the dead.

After the mummy, its coffins, sarcophagus, and covering shrines, the most important among the funeral appurtenances was the Canopic equipment for the viscera. The Canopic chest had on its four corners the four guardian goddesses carved in high relief—Isis on the southwest corner, Nephthys on the northwest corner, Neith on the southeast, and Selkit on the northeast. The interior of the chest was carved out only five inches deep, but sufficiently to give the appearance of four rectangular compartments each containing a jar. Covering the tops of each of the imitation jars were separate human-headed lids, finely sculptured in alabaster in the likeness of the king. The two jars on the east side faced west, and the two on the west side faced east. In each hollow, wrapped in linen, was an exquisite miniature gold coffin which held the viscera, elaborately inlaid and resembling the second coffin of the king. The coffins were placed upright, facing in the same direction as the alabaster lids. These miniature coffins are wonderful specimens of both goldsmith's and jeweler's art.

But in spite of all this care and costly expenditure to preserve and protect the mortal remains of the young king, the sumptuous funerary equipment, and what must have been elaborate funerary rites at the time of entombment, we find gross carelessness on the part of those people who undertook the burial rites.

The ancient Egyptians must have known better than we do now that the goddess Nephthys should be on the south side of the chest, and that her charge was the genius Hepy and that Selkit should be on the east side, and her charge was the genius Qebeh-sne wef. Yet in erecting this Canopic equipment, even though it bears distinct marks as well as distinguishing inscriptions upon each side, they place Selkit south in the place of Nephthys, and Nephthys east

Interior of the Innermost Treasury

128

where Selkit should have been. Moreover, the carpenters who put together the sections of the canopy and fitted the wooden covering over the alabaster chest left their refuse (wood chips) in a heap on the floor of the chamber.

There was a flotilla of model craft. These models were made of logs of wood, pinned together, shaped and planed with the adze. They are painted and gilded and in some instances highly decorated with brilliant ornamentation. Two had been overturned by the thieves. The remainder of the craft were discovered in the Annex—unfortunately these were almost entirely broken up by plunderers.

Among these crafts were ships to follow the voyage of the sun; canoes for hunting the hippopotamus and fowling in the hereafter, symbolizing the mythical pastimes of Horus in the marshes; vessels for the holy pilgrimage to and from Abydos; and craft to render the deceased independent of the favors of the "celestial ferrymen" to reach the "fields of the blessed," that are surrounded by seething waters difficult to traverse.

On the north side of the room was a row of treasure caskets and plain white boxes. Unfortunately this group had been attacked by the dynastic tomb plunderers for the gold and silver articles that they contained. Their seals were broken, their contents ransacked, their pieces of greater value stolen.

At least 60 per cent of the original contents was missing from these boxes. What was left of the jewelry comprises: some earrings, a necklace, a number of pectoral ornaments, some bracelets and a ring. There were also a lid of a small openwork jeweled box, some scepters, two mirror cases, the residue of some vestments, and a writing outfit—forty-three pieces in all. The exact amount of jewelery taken is impossible to estimate, but we can tell that two mirrors and at least twenty vessels from two of the caskets, four of which are stated to have been of gold, were stolen.

The "sergeants of the necropolis," who reclosed the tomb after the raid, seem to have carried out their duty in a careless and perfunctory manner. What was left had evidently been gathered up and put back into the caskets regardless of the original order. We found parts of an ornament in one casket, parts in another, and the whole mass in confusion.

There was more than enough to enable us to study the skill of the jeweler, as well as the goldsmith's work in the royal workshops of the late Eighteenth Dynasty.

The metals employed were gold, electrum, silver and, in a lesser degree, bronze; the natural stones were amethyst, turquoise, lapis lazuli, calcite, carnelian, chalcedony, green felspar, semitranslucent and translucent quartz (often backed with pigment for brilliance and imitative effects), serpentine, and an obscure hard olive-green stone not identified. In addition to these were composite materials such as faience (glazed pottery), hard vitreous paste, and semitranslucent and opaque colored glasses, used in the place of some one or other of the above-mentioned stones. But perhaps the most remarkable material used in the composition of this jewelery was a dark colored resin, both on ornaments and as beads. Another peculiarity in these ornaments is a brilliant scarlet-tinted gold. This, when overlaid with bright yellow gold ornamentation, such as the granulated goldwork, and in combination with the dark colored resin, imparted a strange and somewhat barbaric effect.

The theme employed in these ornaments has in great part some subordinate connection with the state religion. Of these designs Re, the sun god, and Aah (Thoth), the Moon god, are the nucleus, if not the principal.

With the ancient Egyptians, especially at this moment, there was no god of higher standing than Re. They regarded him as the Master of the Universe, who, from his sacred barque in the heavens, governed all things. To speak of God was to think of Re. Re, the sun itself, "Lord of Heaven," "The Sovereign King of all Life," takes many forms in this jewelery, such as Khepre, Horus, Herakhte, and Atum, each being a local representative of some phase of the sun. Khepre, the scarab, is a transformation of the sun god in the form of the famous dung-beetle. It was in this form that the newly born sun issues from the "Cavern of Dawn" to begin his diurnal career. On his awakening in the East he enters into the morning barque to ascend the heavenly vault, when he is identified with Horus, either as a youth or as a Hobby falcon. A prayer refers to Re with these words: "Beautiful is Thine awakening, O Horus, who voyagest over the sky. . . . The fire-child with glittering rays, dispelling darkness and gloom." As he triumphantly hovers in midair, he is conceived as a great disk with multicolored wings ready to pounce upon his foe. During his heavenly course he also takes the shape of Herakhte, either as a falcon-headed man, or as a peregrine falcon, a highly courageous bird of prey that kills its quarry upon the wing. Finally he becomes the old man, Atum, "the Closer of the Day," enters into the evening barque, and descends behind Manun, the sacred Mountain of the West, into the underworld to begin again his nocturnal journey through the twelve caverns—the hours of the night. There, he gives light to the great god Osiris, "the Ruler of Eternity."

From such mythological considerations as these, there can be little doubt that Pharaonic jewelery was looked upon as sacred. The Egyptians may have believed it to possess magic powers; it may be, too, that priestly orders attached to the court had special charge of it. Underlying its themes of design there certainly appears to lurk an ulterior idea. Thus we find these jewels of Tut-ankh-Amen, though perhaps made for daily use, designed so as to serve a purpose in the world to come.

We found earrings among this jewelery which seem to have belonged to Tut-ankh-Amen in his earlier youth.

When examining the mummy of Tut-ankh-Amen, it was found that his ear lobes were pierced, but among the numerous ornaments that we discovered within his wrappings there was nothing of the nature of an earring. The gold portrait mask that covered his head also had pierced ear lobes, but the holes had been carefully filled in with small disks of thin sheet gold, suggesting an endeavor to hide the fact. Among the representations of kings upon monuments, pierced ear lobes are often marked, but I am not aware of any instance of actual earrings being depicted on a king's ears.

Perhaps the most important objects among this collection of jewelry are the insignia of royalty: the two crozier scepters and two flagella. The crozier, or kind of pastoral staff, was one of the insignia of Osiris. It was held in the left hand of both the god and the king. It takes the form of a short staff ending at the top in a crook bent inward and outward. In this case it is made up of sections of gold, dark blue glass, and obsidian, upon a bronze core.

The flagellum, a kind of whip or scourge commonly known as the "flail," was the complement to the crozier scepter and the second of the insignia proper of Osiris. It was held by both the god and the king in the right hand. It consists of a short handle, bent at an acute angle at the top, to which are attached three "swingles" by means of beaded thongs, in such a manner as to enable them to swing freely. The larger flagellum bears the prenomen and nomen of Tut-ankh-Amen; the smaller one bears his Aten name in place of the Amen name, suggesting that it belonged to the earlier part of the young king's reign before he was converted to the worship of Amen. Its smaller size is also in keeping with this hypothesis. It becomes evident that these insignia were symbols of authority over the two principal factions in early times; the husbandmen and the shepherds.

The numerous sepulchral statuettes called *Shawabti*-figures, representing

Pectoral ornament

the king swathed in linen, are mummiform. Such figures were originally made of *Shawabti* wood whence they derive their name; and their function, according to the sixth chapter of the Book of the Dead, was to act as substitute for the deceased in the netherworld, if he be called upon to perform any fatiguing duties.

Their implements—the hoe, the pick, the yoke, basket, and water vessel— either depicted upon the figures or placed with them as copper and faience models, clearly indicate the duty which they were supposed to perform for their deceased lord in the future life.

Related to the *Shawabti*-figures and reminiscent of Osiris we also found in this room a kind of miniature effigy of the dead king in a small oblong chest, carefully padded with linen.

This effigy was made by Maya, the Overseer of the Works in the Place of Eternity (that is, the tomb). Maya was in all probability responsible for the excavation of the king's tomb, and it is possible that he was also responsible for the resealing of Tut-ankh-Amen's tomb.

Placed on the top of the kiosks of *Shawabti*-figures was a small wooden anthropoid coffin, about thirty inches in length, fashioned like a coffin for a noble of the period. It contained a second coffin of gesso-gilt wood, ornamented after the fashion of a royal coffin, but neither of these two coffins bore royal emblems, although the formulas inscribed upon them give the names of Tut-ankh-Amen. The second coffin contained a third small plain wood coffin, and, beside it, a solid gold statuette of Amen-hetep III rolled up in a separate piece of mummy cloth. Within this third coffin was a fourth, also made of wood, man-shaped, but not more than five inches in length. This last coffin was wrapped in linen, tied at the neck with a band of minute beadwork, sealed at the ankles, and profusely annointed with unguents. It bore the titles and name of Queen Tyi, and, within it, carefully folded in linen, was a plaited lock of her hair.

Such heirlooms as these—a lock of auburn hair of the Great Hereditary Princess, the Great Royal Wife, the Lady of the Two Lands, Tyi, and a statuette of her sovereign husband, Amen-hetep III—are evidence of devotion. They were probably pieces of personal property that had been descending by due succession in the family. Tut-ankh-Amen, the ultimate heir, was the last of that ruling Amen-hetep house; hence these heirlooms were buried with him. The gold statuette suspended on a chain was a trinket and was

Wooden Shawabti-*figures of the king*

treated as such; the lock of hair was human, the remains of a royal personage, and therefore it received the prerogative of a royal burial.

But even more extraordinary were the contents of two miniature anthropoid coffins that were placed, head to foot, in a wooden box beside the above-mentioned coffins. These were also fashioned in the manner such as would be used for a high personage. Each contained an inner gilt coffin of similar design. In one of them was a small mummy, preserved in accordance with burial custom of the Eighteenth Dynasty. It had a gesso-gilt mask (several sizes too large for it) covering its head. The linen wrappings enveloped a well-preserved mummy of a stillborn child. The other contained a slightly larger mummy of a child of premature birth, also wrapped in the prescribed fashion of the period.

There is little doubt that these pathetic remains were the offspring of Tut-ankh-Amen, and, probably, the issue of Ankh-es-en-Amen. Possibly, these *two* premature births were due merely to chance; the outcome of an abnormality of the young queen. However, it must not be forgotten that an accident to the expectant mother would have rendered the throne vacant for those eager to step in.

As I have mentioned, the coffins were placed side by side, head to feet, in a box. We noted with interest that the toes of the foot of the larger coffin had been hacked off because they prevented the lid of the box from closing properly, as had occurred in the case of the king's outer coffin. Another curious fact lies in the absence of a mask over the mummy of the larger child. In the cache discovered by Theodore M. Davis, where remnants from the burial ceremonies of Tut-ankh-Amen were found, there was a gesso-gilt mask of similar dimensions and character to that found here on the smaller child. Could it be that it was intended for this larger mummy, and was omitted because it was too small to fit over the head?

In the northwest corner of this chamber, leaning against the wall, was the king's bow case, the principal theme of ornament being idealized hunting scenes in which the king is the central figure. Toward the tapering ends of the case, which terminate in violet faience heads of cheetahs with gilded manes, are small symbolic scenes where the king, represented as a human-headed lion, tramples upon Egypt's alien foes. The central panels, of embossed gold, represent the king in his chariot, hunting with bow and arrow, accompanied by his hounds, depicted running beside or in front of his steeds, barking, or harassing the quarry. The triangular panels on either side represent various fauna—denizens of the desert—stricken by the king's arrows.

This bow case evidently belonged to one of the king's hunting chariots that were found dismantled in this room, to which it was fastened by means of copper attachments expressly made for the purpose. It contained three neatly made composite bows.

With the dismembered parts of two hunting chariots found in this chamber, was a whip bearing an inscription: "The King's son, Captain of the Troops, Thothmes." Who was this royal prince who, to have been "Captain of the Troops," during the reign of Tut-ankh-Amen could not have been very young? Was he a son of Thothmes IV or of Amen-hetep III? That problem has yet to be solved. If he was a son of Thothmes IV, and was living at the time of Tut-ankh-Amen's burial, he must have reached the age of at least sixty; whereas if he was a son of Amen-hetep III, he could not have been more than thirty-five at the time of Tut-ankh-Amen's death.

The Annex

During the last days of November, 1927, we were able to begin the final stage of our investigations, the clearing of the Annex.

The doorway of the Annex, only fifty-one inches high and thirty-seven inches wide, had been blocked with rough splinters of limestone and was plastered over on the outside. The plaster, while still wet, had received numerous impressions of four different sepulchral seals of the king. Now only the upper part of the blocking remained, the thieves having broken through the lower portion. It was through this hole that we made our first inspection of the room.

The room, comparatively small—fourteen feet long, eight feet, six inches wide, and eight feet, five inches high—gave no suggestion of any kind of finish, nor paid any tribute to taste. It is roughly cut out of the bedrock, and was intended for its purpose—a storeroom.

In contrast to the comparative order and harmony of the contents of the Innermost Treasury, we found in this last chamber a jumble of every kind of funerary article, tumbled any which way, almost defying description. Bedsteads, chairs, stools, footstools, hassocks, game boards, baskets of fruit, every kind of alabaster vessel and pottery wine jar, boxes of funerary figures, toys, shields, bows and arrows, and other missiles, all turned topsy-turvy. Caskets thrown over, their contents spilled; in fact, everything in confusion.

Doubtless this confusion was the work of plunderers, but in the other chambers there had been a perfunctory attempt to restore order. The responsibility for this utter neglect would therefore seem to rest a good deal on the necropolis officials, who, in their task to put to rights the Antechamber, the Burial Chamber, and the Innermost Treasury after the robbery, had neglected this little room altogether.

While contemplating the picture of mingled rapacity and destruction, we could visualize the robbers' hurried scramble for loot—gold and other metals were their natural quarry; everything else they seem to have treated in the most brutal fashion. There was hardly an object that did not bear marks of plundering and before us—upon one of the larger boxes—were the very footprints of the last intruder.

Traces of the dilapidations of time were visible; the rock-cut walls and ceiling were discolored by damp arising from infrequent saturations. Our electric lamps threw a mass of light on the room's crowded contents, bringing out many odd features in strong relief. Close to us, upside down, was a large chair like a folding stool, decorated in the taste of a distant age. Stretching across the room and resting precariously on their sides were bedsteads of a form still used today in the regions of the Upper Nile. Here a vase, and there a tiny figure gazed at one with forlorn expression. There were weapons of various kinds, baskets, pottery and alabaster jars, and gaming boards crushed and mingled with stones that had fallen from the hole that had been forced through the sealed doorway. In an opposite corner, poised high up, as if in a state of indecision, was a broken box bulging with delicate faience vessels, ready to collapse at any moment. In the midst of this miscellany a cabinet upon slender legs stood almost unscathed. Wedged between boxes and under objects of many shapes, were a boat of alabaster, a lion, and a figure of a bleating ibex. A fan, a sandal, a fragment of a robe, a glove keeping odd company with emblems of the living and of the dead. In fact the scene, seemed almost as if contrived with theatrical artifice to bewilder the beholder.

The method we finally adopted to remove those three-hundred-odd pieces of antiquity was somewhat prosaic. To begin with, sufficient floor space had to be made for our feet, and that had to be done as best we could, heads downward, bending over the doorsill, which was more than three feet above the floor level. While carrying out this uncomfortable operation, we had to take every precaution lest a hasty movement should cause an avalanche of antiquities precariously piled up and beyond our reach. Often, to save a heavy object so situated that the slightest disturbance would cause it to fall, we were obliged to lean over and reach far out, supported by a rope-sling under our armpits, held by three or four men standing in the Antechamber. In that manner, by always removing one by one the uppermost objects in reach, we gained entrance and gradually collected the treasures. Each object, or group of objects, had first to be photographed, numbered, and recorded, before it was moved.

I must confess that my first impression was that the positions of those objects were meaningless, and that there was little or nothing to be learned from such disorder. But as we proceeded in our investigations, it became evident that much data could be gleaned as to their original order and subsequent chaos. Careful examination of the facts disclosed one important point: two separate thefts of quite different nature had taken place in that little apartment. The first theft—for gold, silver, and bronze—was perpetrated by the famous tomb metal robbers, who ransacked the four chambers of the tomb for all such portable material. The second robbery was evidently by another class of thief, who sought only the costly oils and unguents contained in the numerous stone vessels. It also became clear that this Annex was intended for a storeroom for housing oils, unguents, wine, and food, like the similar small chambers in other royal tombs of the Eighteenth Dynasty. But in this case an overflow of other material belonging to the burial equipment had been stacked on top of the room's proper contents.

The material that might be termed extraneous was probably put there, not so much for lack of space elsewhere, but probably owing to the absence of system when the equipment was being placed in the tomb. For example, below the Hathor couch in the Antechamber there was a pile of uniform wooden cases containing a variety of meats. Those should have been stored in the Annex. But owing to some oversight they seem to have been forgotten, and, the doorway of the Annex having been closed, they had to be put in some convenient place in the Antechamber, which, in natural sequence, was the last room of the tomb to be closed. Also, part of the series of funerary boats and figures (*shawabtis*), placed in the Innermost Treasury were found in this Annex.

Alabaster boat

From the facts gleaned we may reconstruct the sequence of events that took place: firstly, nearly forty pottery wine jars were placed on the floor at the northern end of the Annex; next to these were added at least thirty-five heavy alabaster vessels containing oils and unguents; stacked beside them, some even on top, were 116 baskets of fruit; the remaining space was then used for furniture—boxes, stools, chairs, and bedsteads—that were piled on top of them. The doorway was then closed and sealed. This was carried out before any material was placed in the Antechamber, since nothing could have been passed into this Annex, nor could the doorway have been closed, after the introduction of the materials belonging to the Antechamber.

When the metal robbers made their first incursion, they evidently crept under the Thueris couch in the Antechamber, forced their way through the sealed doorway of the Annex, ransacked its entire contents for portable metal objects, and were, no doubt, responsible for a great deal of the disorder found in that chamber. Subsequently—it is impossible to say when—a second robbery took place. Its objective was the costly oils and unguents contained in the alabaster jars. This last robbery had been carefully thought out. The stone vessels being far too heavy and cumbersome to carry away, the thieves came provided with some more convenient receptacles, such as leather bags or water skins, to take away the spoil. There was not a stopper of a jar that had not been removed, not a jar that had not been emptied. The fingerprints of those thieves are visible today on the interior walls of some of the vessels that had contained viscous ointments. To get at those heavy stone vessels, the furniture piled on top of them was evidently turned over and thrown helter-skelter from side to side.

The knowledge of this second robbery throws light upon a problem that had puzzled us ever since the beginning of the discovery of the tomb. Why, throughout its funerary equipment, had quite insignificant stone vessels been tampered with? Why were some of them left empty lying on the floors of the chambers, and others taken out and discarded in the entrance passage? The greases or oils that they once contained had no doubt a far greater value in those days than possibly we imagine. It also explains why the tomb was twice reclosed, as traces on the sealed entrances and inner doorway of the passage signified. I believe also that the odd baskets and simple alabaster jars that were found scattered on the floor of the Antechamber came from the group in the Annex. They are obviously of the same class and were probably taken out for convenience by the thieves. The same argument holds true of the solitary *Shawabti*-figure discovered leaning against the north wall of the Antechamber. It surely came from one of the broken *Shawabti*-boxes in the Annex—for others like it were found there.

Tradition holds that in burial custom each article belonging to tomb equipment had its prescribed place in the tomb. However, no matter how true the governing conventions may be, seldom were they strictly carried out. Either the lack of forethought with regard to space, or the lack of system when placing the elaborate paraphernalia in the tomb chambers overcame tradition. We have never found any strict order, we have found only approximate order.

We have found evidence in this tomb of love and respect mingled with want of order and eventual dishonor. This tomb, though it did not wholly share the fate of its kindred, though mightier, mausoleums, was nevertheless robbed— twice robbed—in pharaonic times. Both robberies probably took place within a few years after the burial. The transfer of Akh-en-Aten's mummy from its original tomb at Tell el-Amarna to its rock-cut cell at Thebes, apparently within the reign of Tut-ankh-Amen, and the renewal of the burial of Thothmes IV, in the eighth year of the reign of Hor-em-heb, after his tomb had been robbed of its treasures, throw considerable light upon the state of affairs in the royal necropolis at that age. The religious confusion of the state at that time; the collapse of the Eighteenth Dynasty; the retention of the throne by the Grand Chamberlain and probably Regent, Ay, who was eventually supplanted by General Hor-em-heb, were incidents which we may assume helped toward such forms of pillage. It must have been a considerable time before even the conquering Hor-em-heb was able to restore order out of the confusion that existed at that period, establish his kingdom, and enforce the law of his state. In any case, the evidence afforded by those two burials and by this tomb prove how the royal tombs suffered even within their own dynasties. The wonder is that Tut-ankh-Amen's tomb, this royal burial with all its riches, escaped the eventual fate of the twenty-seven others in the Valley.

Page 144: *Gold amulet from the king's neck*